MznLnx

Missing Links Exam Preps

Exam Prep for

Financial management for Public, Health and Not-For-Profit Organizations

Finkler, 2nd Edition

The MznLnx Exam Prep is your link from the texbook and lecture to your exams.
The MznLnx Exam Preps are unauthorized and comprehensive reviews of your textbooks.

All material provided by MznLnx and Rico Publications (c) 2010
Textbook publishers and textbook authors do not particpate in or contribute to these reviews.

MznLnx

Rico Publications

Exam Prep for Financial management for Public, Health and Not-For-Profit Organizations
2nd Edition
Finkler

Publisher: Raymond Houge
Assistant Editor: Michael Rouger
Text and Cover Designer: Lisa Buckner
Marketing Manager: Sara Swagger
Project Manager, Editorial Production: Jerry Emerson
Art Director: Vernon Lowerui

Product Manager: Dave Mason
Editorial Assitant: Rachel Guzmanji
Pedagogy: Debra Long
Cover Image: Jim Reed/Getty Images
Text and Cover Printer: City Printing, Inc.
Compositor: Media Mix, Inc.

(c) 2010 Rico Publications
ALL RIGHTS RESERVED. No part of this work covered by the copyright may be reproduced or used in any form or by an means--graphic, electronic, or mechanical, including photocopying, recording, taping, Web distribution, information storage, and retrieval systems, or in any other manner--without the written permission of the publisher.

Printed in the United States
ISBN:

For more information about our products, contact us at:
Dave.Mason@RicoPublications.com

For permission to use material from this text or product, submit a request online to:
Dave.Mason@RicoPublications.com

Contents

CHAPTER 1
Introduction to Financial Management   1

CHAPTER 2
Planning for Success: Budgeting   6

CHAPTER 3
Additional Budgeting Concepts   13

CHAPTER 4
Understanding Costs   23

CHAPTER 5
Capital Budgeting and Long-Term Financing   28

CHAPTER 6
Managing Short-Term Resources and Obligations   43

CHAPTER 7
Accountability and Control   53

CHAPTER 8
Taking Stock of Where You Are: The Balance Sheet   57

CHAPTER 9
Reporting the Results of Operations: The Activity and Cash Flow Statements   74

CHAPTER 10
Unique Aspects of Accounting for Not-for-Profit and Health Care Organizations   84

CHAPTER 11
Unique Aspects of Accounting for State and Local Governments   89

CHAPTER 12
Financial Statement Analysis   98

CHAPTER 13
Financial Condition Analysis   108

ANSWER KEY   114

TO THE STUDENT

COMPREHENSIVE

The *MznLnx* Exam Prep series is designed to help you pass your exams. Editors at MznLnx review your textbooks and then prepare these practice exams to help you master the textbook material. Unlike study guides, workbooks, and practice tests provided by the texbook publisher and textbook authors, *MznLnx* gives you **all** of the material in each chapter in exam form, not just samples, so you can be sure to nail your exam.

MECHANICAL

The MznLnx Exam Prep series creates exams that will help you learn the subject matter as well as test you on your understanding. Each question is designed to help you master the concept. Just working through the exams, you gain an understanding of the subject--its a simple mechanical process that produces success.

INTEGRATED STUDY GUIDE AND REVIEW

MznLnx is not just a set of exams designed to test you, its also a comprehensive review of the subject content. Each exam question is also a review of the concept, making sure that you will get the answer correct without having to go to other sources of material. You learn as you go! Its the easiest way to pass an exam.

HUMOR

Studying can be tedious and dry. MznLnx's instructional design includes moderate humor within the exam questions on occassion, to break the tedium and revitalize the brain

Chapter 1. Introduction to Financial Management

1. A _____ is a party (e.g. person, organization, company, or government) that has a claim to the services of a second party. The first party, in general, has provided some property or service to the second party under the assumption (usually enforced by contract) that the second party will return an equivalent property or service. The second party is frequently called a debtor or borrower.
   a. False billing
   b. NOPLAT
   c. Redemption value
   d. Creditor

2. _____ or First In, First Out, is an abstraction in ways of organizing and manipulation of data relative to time and prioritization. This expression describes the principle of a queue processing technique or servicing conflicting demands by ordering process by first-come, first-served (FCFS) behaviour: what comes in first is handled first, what comes in next waits until the first is finished, etc.

   Thus it is analogous to the behaviour of persons queueing (or 'standing in line', in common American parlance), where the persons leave the queue in the order they arrive, or waiting one's turn at a traffic control signal.

   a. 4-4-5 Calendar
   b. Risk management
   c. Penny stock
   d. FIFO

3. _____ is the field of accountancy concerned with the preparation of financial statements for decision makers, such as stockholders, suppliers, banks, employees, government agencies, owners, and other stakeholders. The fundamental need for _____ is to reduce principal-agent problem by measuring and monitoring agents' performance and reporting the results to interested users.

   _____ is used to prepare accounting information for people outside the organization or not involved in the day to day running of the company.

   a. 4-4-5 Calendar
   b. 529 plan
   c. 7-Eleven
   d. Financial accounting

4. _____ is concerned with the provisions and use of accounting information to managers within organizations, to provide them with the basis to make informed business decisions that will allow them to be better equipped in their management and control functions.

In contrast to financial accountancy information, _____ information is:

- usually confidential and used by management, instead of publicly reported;
- forward-looking, instead of historical;
- pragmatically computed using extensive management information systems and internal controls, instead of complying with accounting standards.

This is because of the different emphasis: _____ information is used within an organization, typically for decision-making.

According to the Chartered Institute of Management Accountants, _____ is 'the process of identification, measurement, accumulation, analysis, preparation, interpretation and communication of information used by management to plan, evaluate and control within an entity and to assure appropriate use of and accountability for its Resource (economics)resources. _____ also comprises the preparation of financial reports for non-management groups such as shareholders, creditors, regulatory agencies and tax authorities'.

   a. Grenzplankostenrechnung
   b. Nonassurance services
   c. Governmental accounting
   d. Management accounting

5. The _____ is one of the measures of national income and input for a given country's economy. _____ is defined as the total cost of all finished goods and services produced within the country in a stipulated period of time (usually a 365-day year.) It is sometimes regarded as the sum of profits added at every level of production (the intermediate stages) of all final goods and services produced within a country in a stipulated timeframe, and it is rarely given a monetary value.
   a. Recession
   b. Macroeconomics
   c. Gross domestic product
   d. Behavioral finance

6. In economics, an _____ or spillover of an economic transaction is an impact on a party that is not directly involved in the transaction. In such a case, prices do not reflect the full costs or benefits in production or consumption of a product or service. A positive impact is called an external benefit, while a negative impact is called an external cost.
   a. ABN Amro
   b. AAB
   c. A Random Walk Down Wall Street
   d. Externality

Chapter 1. Introduction to Financial Management

7. In a company, _____ is the sum of all financial records of salaries, wages, bonuses and deductions.

A paycheck, is traditionally a paper document issued by an employer to pay an employee for services rendered. While most commonly used in the United States, recently the physical paycheck has been increasingly replaced by electronic direct deposit to bank accounts.

   a. 529 plan
   b. Tax expense
   c. Payroll
   d. 4-4-5 Calendar

8. _____ generally refers to two kinds of taxes: Taxes which employers are required to withhold from employees' pay Pay-As-You-Earn or Pay-As-You-Go tax; and taxes which are paid from the employer's own funds and which are directly related to employing a worker, which may be either fixed charges or proportionally linked to an employee's pay.

In China, the _____ is a specific tax which is paid to states and territories by employers, not by employees. The tax is not deducted from the worker's pay.

   a. Capital gain
   b. Tax brackets
   c. Withholding tax
   d. Payroll Tax

9. A _____ (or financial year, or sometimes budget year) is a period used for calculating annual ('yearly') financial statements in businesses and other organizations. In many jurisdictions, regulatory laws regarding accounting and taxation require such reports once per twelve months, but do not require that the period reported on constitutes a calendar year (i.e., January through December.) _____s vary between businesses and countries.

   a. Fiscal year
   b. Special journals
   c. Matching principle
   d. Purchase ledger

10. _____, refers to consumption opportunity gained by an entity within a specified time frame, which is generally expressed in monetary terms. However, for households and individuals, '_____ is the sum of all the wages, salaries, profits, interests payments, rents and other forms of earnings received... in a given period of time.' For firms, _____ generally refers to net-profit: what remains of revenue after expenses have been subtracted.

a. Annual report
b. OIBDA
c. Accrual
d. Income

11. An _____ is a tax levied on the financial income of people, corporations, or other legal entities. Various _____ systems exist, with varying degrees of tax incidence. Income taxation can be progressive, proportional, or regressive.
   a. AAB
   b. ABN Amro
   c. A Random Walk Down Wall Street
   d. Income tax

12. _____ is that which is owed; usually referencing assets owed, but the term can cover other obligations. In the case of assets, _____ is a means of using future purchasing power in the present before a summation has been earned. Some companies and corporations use _____ as a part of their overall corporate finance strategy.
   a. Credit cycle
   b. Debt
   c. Cross-collateralization
   d. Partial Payment

13. A _____ is a fungible, negotiable instrument representing financial value. They are broadly categorized into debt securities (such as banknotes, bonds and debentures), and equity securities; e.g., common stocks. The company or other entity issuing the _____ is called the issuer.
   a. Securities lending
   b. Book entry
   c. Tracking stock
   d. Security

14. _____ is a legally declared inability or impairment of ability of an individual or organization to pay their creditors. Creditors may file a _____ petition against a debtor ('involuntary _____') in an effort to recoup a portion of what they are owed or initiate a restructuring. In the majority of cases, however, _____ is initiated by the debtor (a 'voluntary _____' that is filed by the bankrupt individual or organization.)

a. Bankruptcy
b. Debt settlement
c. 529 plan
d. 4-4-5 Calendar

15. _____ is the difference between price and the costs of bringing to market whatever it is that is accounted as an enterprise (whether by harvest, extraction, manufacture, or purchase) in terms of the component costs of delivered goods and/or services and any operating or other expenses.

A key difficulty in measuring profit is in defining costs. Pure economic monetary profits can be zero or negative even in competitive equilibrium when accounted monetized costs exceed monetized price.

a. AAB
b. Economic profit
c. A Random Walk Down Wall Street
d. Accounting profit

16. The phrase _____ refers to the aspect of corporate strategy, corporate finance and management dealing with the buying, selling and combining of different companies that can aid, finance, or help a growing company in a given industry grow rapidly without having to create another business entity.

An acquisition, also known as a takeover, is the buying of one company (the 'target') by another. An acquisition may be friendly or hostile.

a. 529 plan
b. 7-Eleven
c. 4-4-5 Calendar
d. Mergers and acquisitions

17. A _____ is an exchange of promises between two or more parties to do an act which is enforceable in a court of law. It is where an unqualified offer meets a qualified acceptance and the parties reach Consensus ad Idem. The parties must have the necessary capacity to _____ and the _____ must not be either trifling, indeterminate, impossible or illegal.

a. 529 plan
b. Contract
c. 7-Eleven
d. 4-4-5 Calendar

Chapter 2. Planning for Success: Budgeting

1. A _____ is a brief written statement of the purpose of a company or organization. Ideally, a _____ guides the actions of the organization, spells out its overall goal, provides a sense of direction, and guides decision making for all levels of management.

_____s often contain the following:

- Purpose and aim of the organization
- The organization's primary stakeholders: clients, stockholders, etc.
- Responsibilities of the organization toward these stakeholders
- Products and services offered

In developing a _____:

- Encourage as much input as feasible from employees, volunteers, and other stakeholders
- Publicize it broadly

The _____ can be used to resolve differences between business stakeholders. Stakeholders include: employees including managers and executives, stockholders, board of directors, customers, suppliers, distributors, creditors, governments (local, state, federal, etc.), unions, competitors, NGO's, and the general public.

   a. 529 plan
   b. 4-4-5 Calendar
   c. 7-Eleven
   d. Mission statement

2. In business, _____ is income that a company receives from its normal business activities, usually from the sale of goods and services to customers. Some companies also receive _____ from interest, dividends or royalties paid to them by other companies. _____ may refer to business income in general, or it may refer to the amount, in a monetary unit, received during a period of time, as in 'Last year, Company X had _____ of $32 million.'

In many countries, including the UK, _____ is referred to as turnover.

   a. Furniture, Fixtures and Equipment
   b. Revenue
   c. Matching principle
   d. Bottom line

3. _____ is the difference between price and the costs of bringing to market whatever it is that is accounted as an enterprise (whether by harvest, extraction, manufacture, or purchase) in terms of the component costs of delivered goods and/or services and any operating or other expenses.

Chapter 2. Planning for Success: Budgeting 7

A key difficulty in measuring profit is in defining costs. Pure economic monetary profits can be zero or negative even in competitive equilibrium when accounted monetized costs exceed monetized price.

a. Economic profit
b. A Random Walk Down Wall Street
c. AAB
d. Accounting profit

4. In finance, the value of an option consists of two components, its intrinsic value and its _____. Time value is simply the difference between option value and intrinsic value. _____ is also known as theta, extrinsic value, or instrumental value.
a. Debt buyer
b. Global Squeeze
c. Conservatism
d. Time value

5. Simply put, _____ is the value of money figuring in a given amount of interest for a given amount of time. For example 100 dollars of todays money held for a year at 5 percent interest is worth 105 dollars, therefore 100 dollars paid now or 105 dollars paid exactly one year from now is the same amount of payment of money with that given intersest at that given amount of time. This notion dates at least to Martín de Azpilcueta of the School of Salamanca.

All of the standard calculations for _____ derive from the most basic algebraic expression for the present value of a future sum, 'discounted' to the present by an amount equal to the _____. For example, a sum of FV to be received in one year is discounted (at the rate of interest r) to give a sum of PV at present: PV = FV -- rÂ·PV = FV/(1+r).

a. Current account
b. Zero-coupon bond
c. Coefficient of variation
d. Time value of money

6. _____ is the planning process used to determine whether a firm's long term investments such as new machinery, replacement machinery, new plants, new products, and research development projects are worth pursuing. It is budget for major capital, or investment, expenditures.

Many formal methods are used in _____, including the techniques such as

- Net present value
- Profitability index
- Internal rate of return
- Modified Internal Rate of Return
- Equivalent annuity

These methods use the incremental cash flows from each potential investment, or project. Techniques based on accounting earnings and accounting rules are sometimes used - though economists consider this to be improper - such as the accounting rate of return, and 'return on investment.' Simplified and hybrid methods are used as well, such as payback period and discounted payback period.

a. Preferred stock
b. Shareholder value
c. Financial distress
d. Capital budgeting

7. Working capital requirements of a business should be monitored at all times to ensure that there are sufficient funds available to meet short-term expenses.

The _____ is basically a detailed plan that shows all expected sources and uses of cash

a. Mitigating Control
b. Loans and interest, in Judaism
c. Rate of return
d. Cash budget

8. A _____ an audit of financial statements, is the review of the financial statements of a company or any other legal entity (including governments), resulting in the publication of an independent opinion on whether or not those financial statements are relevant, accurate, complete, and fairly presented.

_____s are typically performed by firms of practicing accountants due to the specialist financial reporting knowledge they require. The _____ is one of many assurance or attestation functions provided by accounting and auditing firms, whereby the firm provides an independent opinion on published information.

Chapter 2. Planning for Success: Budgeting

a. Provided by client
b. Financial audit
c. Joint audit
d. Lead Auditor

9. The phrase _____ refers to the aspect of corporate strategy, corporate finance and management dealing with the buying, selling and combining of different companies that can aid, finance, or help a growing company in a given industry grow rapidly without having to create another business entity.

An acquisition, also known as a takeover, is the buying of one company (the 'target') by another. An acquisition may be friendly or hostile.

a. 529 plan
b. 4-4-5 Calendar
c. 7-Eleven
d. Mergers and acquisitions

10. Two primary accounting methods, _____ and accrual basis, are used to calculate taxable income for U.S. federal income taxes. According to the Internal Revenue Code, a taxpayer may compute taxable income by:

1. the Cash receipts and disbursements method;
2. an accrual method;
3. any other method permitted by the chapter; or
4. any combination of the foregoing methods permitted under regulations prescribed by the Secretary.

As a general rule, a taxpayer must compute taxable income using the same accounting method he uses to compute income in keeping his books. Also, the taxpayer must maintain a consistent method of accounting from year to year. Should he change from the _____ to the accrual basis (or vice versa), he must notify and secure the consent of the Secretary.

a. Cash basis
b. 7-Eleven
c. 4-4-5 Calendar
d. 529 plan

11. A _____ (or financial year, or sometimes budget year) is a period used for calculating annual ('yearly') financial statements in businesses and other organizations. In many jurisdictions, regulatory laws regarding accounting and taxation require such reports once per twelve months, but do not require that the period reported on constitutes a calendar year (i.e., January through December.) _____s vary between businesses and countries.

a. Fiscal year
b. Matching principle
c. Special journals
d. Purchase ledger

12. Accrual, in accounting, describes the accounting method known as _____, whereby revenues and expenses are recognized when they are accrued, i.e. accumulated (earned or incurred), regardless when the actual cash is received or paid out.

E.g. a company delivers a product to a customer who will pay for it 30 days later in the next fiscal year starting a week after the delivery. The company recognizes the proceeds as a revenue in its current income statement still for the fiscal year of the delivery, even though it will get paid in cash during the following accounting period.

a. A Random Walk Down Wall Street
b. ABN Amro
c. Accrual basis
d. AAB

13. _____ is a term used in accounting, economics and finance to spread the cost of an asset over the span of several years.

In simple words we can say that _____ is the reduction in the value of an asset due to usage, passage of time, wear and tear, technological outdating or obsolescence, depletion or other such factors.

In accounting, _____ is a term used to describe any method of attributing the historical or purchase cost of an asset across its useful life, roughly corresponding to normal wear and tear.

a. Bottom line
b. Depreciation
c. Deferred financing costs
d. Matching principle

14. Two primary _____, cash and accrual basis, and their combination, called modified cash basis, are used in recognizing income (revenues) and expenses in bookkeeping in order to measure net income for a specified time interval (accounting period.) Both methods differ on such recognition leading to varying income recordings, which may be subject to error or - manipulation. Many financial scandals involved accounting manipulations.

a. Asset
   b. Outstanding balance
   c. Accounting equation
   d. Accounting methods

15. In business and accounting, _____s are everything of value that is owned by a person or company. The balance sheet of a firm records the monetary value of the _____s owned by the firm. The two major _____ classes are tangible _____s and intangible _____s.
   a. Asset
   b. EBITDA
   c. Accounts payable
   d. Income

16. _____ is a legal term of art for anything that affects or limits the title of a property, such as mortgages, leases, easements, liens, or restrictions. Also, those considered as potentially making the title defeasible are also _____s. For example, charging orders, building orders and structure alteration.
   a. A Random Walk Down Wall Street
   b. ABN Amro
   c. AAB
   d. Encumbrance

17. In accounting and finance, _____ is the portion of receivables that can no longer be collected, typically from accounts receivable or loans. _____ in accounting is considered an expense.

There are two methods to account for _____:

   1. Direct write off method (Non - GAAP)

A receivable which is not considered collectible is charged directly to the income statement.

   1. Allowance method (GAAP)

An estimate is made at the end of each fiscal year of the amount of _____. This is then accumulated in a provision which is then used to reduce specific receivable accounts as and when necessary.

a. 4-4-5 Calendar
b. Tax expense
c. Bad debt
d. 529 plan

18. _____ is that which is owed; usually referencing assets owed, but the term can cover other obligations. In the case of assets, _____ is a means of using future purchasing power in the present before a summation has been earned. Some companies and corporations use _____ as a part of their overall corporate finance strategy.
   a. Cross-collateralization
   b. Credit cycle
   c. Debt
   d. Partial Payment

Chapter 3. Additional Budgeting Concepts

1. _____ is the process of dispersing decision-making governance closer to the people or citizen. It includes the dispersal of administration or governance in sectors or areas like engineering, management science, political science, political economy, sociology and economics. _____ is also possible in the dispersal of population and employment.
   a. Decentralization
   b. Cash cow
   c. Corporate Transparency
   d. Management by exception

2. _____ is the planning process used to determine whether a firm's long term investments such as new machinery, replacement machinery, new plants, new products, and research development projects are worth pursuing. It is budget for major capital, or investment, expenditures.

   Many formal methods are used in _____, including the techniques such as

   - Net present value
   - Profitability index
   - Internal rate of return
   - Modified Internal Rate of Return
   - Equivalent annuity

   These methods use the incremental cash flows from each potential investment, or project. Techniques based on accounting earnings and accounting rules are sometimes used - though economists consider this to be improper - such as the accounting rate of return, and 'return on investment.' Simplified and hybrid methods are used as well, such as payback period and discounted payback period.

   a. Shareholder value
   b. Capital budgeting
   c. Preferred stock
   d. Financial distress

3. _____ or financing is to provide capital (funds), which means money for a project, a person, a business or any other private or public institutions.

   Those funds can be allocated for either short term or long term purposes. The health fund is a new way of _____ private healthcare centers.

   a. Proxy fight
   b. Product life cycle
   c. Synthetic CDO
   d. Funding

Chapter 3. Additional Budgeting Concepts

4. In economic models, the _____ time frame assumes no fixed factors of production. Firms can enter or leave the marketplace, and the cost (and availability) of land, labor, raw materials, and capital goods can be assumed to vary. In contrast, in the short-run time frame, certain factors are assumed to be fixed, because there is not sufficient time for them to change.
   a. 529 plan
   b. 4-4-5 Calendar
   c. Short-run
   d. Long-run

5. In economics, business, and accounting, a _____ is the value of money that has been used up to produce something, and hence is not available for use anymore. In business, the _____ may be one of acquisition, in which case the amount of money expended to acquire it is counted as _____. In this case, money is the input that is gone in order to acquire the thing.
   a. Marginal cost
   b. Cost
   c. Sliding scale fees
   d. Fixed costs

6. _____ are business expenses that are not dependent on the level of production or sales. They tend to be time-related, such as salaries or rents being paid per month. This is in contrast to Variable costs, which are volume-related (and are paid per quantity.)
   a. Fixed costs
   b. Sliding scale fees
   c. Marginal cost
   d. Transaction cost

7. _____ are expenses that change in proportion to the activity of a business. In other words, _____ are the sum of marginal costs. It can also be considered normal costs. Along with fixed costs, _____ make up the two components of total cost. Direct Costs, however, are costs that can be associated with a particular cost object.
   a. Transaction cost
   b. Fixed costs
   c. Cost accounting
   d. Variable costs

8. _____ refers to an examination of a program, function, operation or the management systems and procedures of a governmental or non-profit entity to assess whether the entity is achieving economy, efficiency and effectiveness in the employment of available resources. The examination is objective and systematic, generally using structured and professionally adopted methodologies.

Chapter 3. Additional Budgeting Concepts

In most countries, _____s of governmental activities are carried out by the external audit bodies at federal or state level.

a. Trustworthy Repositories Audit ' Certification
b. Clinical audit
c. Generally Accepted Auditing Standards
d. Performance audit

9. _____ is a term that refers both to:

- a formal discipline used to help appraise, or assess, the case for a project or proposal, which itself is a process known as project appraisal; and
- an informal approach to making decisions of any kind.

Under both definitions the process involves, whether explicitly or implicitly, weighing the total expected costs against the total expected benefits of one or more actions in order to choose the best or most profitable option.

A hallmark of _____ is that all benefits and all costs are expressed in money terms, and are adjusted for the time value of money, so that all flows of benefits and flows of project costs over time (which tend to occur at different points in time) are expressed on a common basis in terms of their present value.

a. Cost-benefit analysis
b. 7-Eleven
c. 4-4-5 Calendar
d. 529 plan

10. _____ or economic opportunity loss is the value of the next best alternative foregone as the result of making a decision. _____ analysis is an important part of a company's decision-making processes but is not treated as an actual cost in any financial statement. The next best thing that a person can engage in is referred to as the _____ of doing the best thing and ignoring the next best thing to be done.

a. ABN Amro
b. Opportunity cost
c. A Random Walk Down Wall Street
d. AAB

11. In economics and finance, _____ is the change in total cost that arises when the quantity produced changes by one unit. It is the cost of producing one more unit of a good. Mathematically, the _____ function is expressed as the first derivative of the total cost (TC) function with respect to quantity (Q). Note that the _____ may change with volume, and so at each level of production, the _____ is the cost of the next unit produced.

Chapter 3. Additional Budgeting Concepts

A typical _____ Curve

a. Sliding scale fees
b. Cost accounting
c. Fixed costs
d. Marginal cost

12. _____ is a technique of planning and decision-making which reverses the working process of traditional budgeting. In traditional incremental budgeting, departmental managers justify only increases over the previous year budget and what has been already spent is automatically sanctioned. No reference is made to the previous level of expenditure.
    a. 529 plan
    b. 4-4-5 Calendar
    c. 7-Eleven
    d. Zero-based budgeting

13. In financial accounting, the term _____ is most commonly used to describe any part of shareholders' equity, except for basic share capital. Sometimes, the term is used instead of the term provision; such a use, however, is inconsistent with the terminology suggested by International Accounting Standards Board. For more information about provisions, see provision (accounting.)
    a. FIFO and LIFO accounting
    b. Reserve
    c. Treasury stock
    d. Closing entries

14. _____ is the balance of the amounts of cash being received and paid by a business during a defined period of time, sometimes tied to a specific project. Measurement of _____ can be used

- to evaluate the state or performance of a business or project.
- to determine problems with liquidity. Being profitable does not necessarily mean being liquid. A company can fail because of a shortage of cash, even while profitable.
- to generate project rate of returns. The time of _____s into and out of projects are used as inputs to financial models such as internal rate of return, and net present value.
- to examine income or growth of a business when it is believed that accrual accounting concepts do not represent economic realities. Alternately, _____ can be used to 'validate' the net income generated by accrual accounting.

Chapter 3. Additional Budgeting Concepts 17

_____ as a generic term may be used differently depending on context, and certain _____ definitions may be adapted by analysts and users for their own uses. Common terms include operating _____ and free _____.

_____s can be classified into:

1. Operational _____s: Cash received or expended as a result of the company's core business activities.
2. Investment _____s: Cash received or expended through capital expenditure, investments or acquisitions.
3. Financing _____s: Cash received or expended as a result of financial activities, such as interests and dividends.

All three together - the net _____ - are necessary to reconcile the beginning cash balance to the ending cash balance. Loan draw downs or equity injections, that is just shifting of capital but no expenditure as such, are not considered in the net _____.

a. Cash flow
b. Shareholder value
c. Real option
d. Corporate finance

15. In financial accounting, a _____ or statement of cash flows is a financial statement that shows a company's flow of cash. The money coming into the business is called cash inflow, and money going out from the business is called cash outflow. The statement shows how changes in balance sheet and income accounts affect cash and cash equivalents, and breaks the analysis down to operating, investing, and financing activities.
   a. 529 plan
   b. 4-4-5 Calendar
   c. Cash flow statement
   d. 7-Eleven

16. In statistics, the _____, R^2 is used in the context of statistical models whose main purpose is the prediction of future outcomes on the basis of other related information. It is the proportion of variability in a data set that is accounted for by the statistical model. It provides a measure of how well future outcomes are likely to be predicted by the model.
   a. 529 plan
   b. 7-Eleven
   c. 4-4-5 Calendar
   d. Coefficient of determination

17. In cost-volume-profit analysis, a form of management accounting, _____ is the marginal profit per unit sale. It is a useful quantity in carrying out various calculations, and can be used as a measure of operating leverage.

The Total _____ is Total Revenue (TR, or Sales) minus Total Variable Cost (TVC):

TContribution margin = TR >− TVC

The Unit _____ (C) is Unit Revenue (Price, P) minus Unit Variable Cost (V):

C = P >− V

The _____ Ratio is the percentage of Contribution over Total Revenue, which can be calculated from the unit contribution over unit price or total contribution over Total Revenue:

>

For instance, if the price is $10 and the unit variable cost is $2, then the unit _____ is $8, and the _____ ratio is $8/$10 = 80%.

a. 529 plan
b. Contribution margin
c. 4-4-5 Calendar
d. 7-Eleven

18. _____ is an acronym which stands for last in, first out. In computer science and queueing theory this refers to the way items stored in some types of data structures are processed. By definition, in a _____ structured linear list, elements can be added or taken off from only one end, called the 'top'.
a. 529 plan
b. 4-4-5 Calendar
c. LIFO
d. 7-Eleven

19. _____ is the value on a given date of a future payment or series of future payments, discounted to reflect the time value of money and other factors such as investment risk. _____ calculations are widely used in business and economics to provide a means to compare cash flows at different times on a meaningful 'like to like' basis.

The most commonly applied model of the time value of money is compound interest.

a. Negative gearing
b. Present value of benefits
c. Net present value
d. Present value

20. _____ measures the rate of return on the ownership interest (shareholders' equity) of the common stock owners. _____ is viewed as one of the most important financial ratios. It measures a firm's efficiency at generating profits from every dollar of shareholders' equity (also known as net assets or assets minus liabilities.)
   a. Return of capital
   b. Return on sales
   c. Diluted Earnings Per Share
   d. Return on equity

21. The _____ percentage shows how profitable a company's assets are in generating revenue.

    _____ can be computed as:

    $$\text{ROA} = \frac{\text{Net Income}}{\text{Total Assets}}$$

    This number tells you 'what the company can do with what it's got', i.e. how many dollars of earnings they derive from each dollar of assets they control. It's a useful number for comparing competing companies in the same industry.

   a. Return on sales
   b. P/E ratio
   c. Receivables turnover ratio
   d. Return on assets

22. In business and accounting, _____s are everything of value that is owned by a person or company. The balance sheet of a firm records the monetary value of the _____s owned by the firm. The two major _____ classes are tangible _____s and intangible _____s.
   a. EBITDA
   b. Income
   c. Accounts payable
   d. Asset

Chapter 3. Additional Budgeting Concepts

23. In probability theory and statistics, _____ indicates the strength and direction of a linear relationship between two random variables. That is in contrast with the usage of the term in colloquial speech, which denotes any relationship, not necessarily linear. In general statistical usage, _____ or co-relation refers to the departure of two random variables from independence.
    a. Variance
    b. Correlation
    c. Geometric mean
    d. Probability distribution

24. In finance, a _____ is collateral that the holder of a position in securities, options, or futures contracts has to deposit to cover the credit risk of his counterparty (most often his broker.) This risk can arise if the holder has done any of the following:

    - borrowed cash from the counterparty to buy securities or options,
    - sold securities or options short, or
    - entered into a futures contract.

    The collateral can be in the form of cash or securities, and it is deposited in a _____ account. On U.S. futures exchanges, '_____' was formally called performance bond.

    _____ buying is buying securities with cash borrowed from a broker, using other securities as collateral.

    a. Share
    b. Credit
    c. Procter ' Gamble
    d. Margin

25. _____ are sometimes the same as net worth, or shareholders' equity - assets minus liabilities. The term _____ is commonly used with charities or not for profit entities. Although these entities don't make money, it is important to maintain reasonable reserves to help future growth.
    a. Sustainable growth rate
    b. Cash conversion cycle
    c. Net assets
    d. Sharpe ratio

26. In statistical hypothesis testing, the _____ is the probability of obtaining a result at least as extreme as the one that was actually observed, given that the null hypothesis is true. The fact that _____s are based on this assumption is crucial to their correct interpretation.

More technically, a _____ of an experiment is a random variable defined over the sample space of the experiment such that its distribution under the null hypothesis is uniform on the interval [0,1].

   a. Median
   b. P-value
   c. Standard score
   d. Standard deviation

27.   In probability theory and statistics, the _____ of a random variable, probability distribution averaging the squared distance of its possible values from the expected value (mean.) Whereas the mean is a way to describe the location of a distribution, the _____ is a way to capture its scale or degree of being spread out. The unit of _____ is the square of the unit of the original variable.
   a. Harmonic mean
   b. Semivariance
   c. Monte Carlo methods
   d. Variance

28.   _____ is a fee paid on borrowed assets. It is the price paid for the use of borrowed money , or, money earned by deposited funds . Assets that are sometimes lent with _____ include money, shares, consumer goods through hire purchase, major assets such as aircraft, and even entire factories in finance lease arrangements.
   a. Insolvency
   b. A Random Walk Down Wall Street
   c. AAB
   d. Interest

29.   In statistics, _____ is used for two things;

   - to construct a simple formula that will predict a value or values for a variable given the value of another variable.
   - to test whether and how a given variable is related to another variable or variables.

_____ is a form of regression analysis in which the relationship between one or more independent variables and another variable, called the dependent variable, is modelled by a least squares function, called a _____ equation. This function is a linear combination of one or more model parameters, called regression coefficients. A _____ equation with one independent variable represents a straight line when the predicted value (i.e. the dependant variable from the regression equation) is plotted against the independent variable: this is called a simple _____. However, note that 'linear' does not refer to this straight line, but rather to the way in which the regression coefficients occur in the regression equation.

a. Stock trader
b. Wall Street Crash of 1929
c. Foreign Language and Area Studies
d. Linear regression

Chapter 4. Understanding Costs

1. In economics, business, and accounting, a _____ is the value of money that has been used up to produce something, and hence is not available for use anymore. In business, the _____ may be one of acquisition, in which case the amount of money expended to acquire it is counted as _____. In this case, money is the input that is gone in order to acquire the thing.
   a. Cost
   b. Sliding scale fees
   c. Marginal cost
   d. Fixed costs

2. _____ or economic opportunity loss is the value of the next best alternative foregone as the result of making a decision. _____ analysis is an important part of a company's decision-making processes but is not treated as an actual cost in any financial statement. The next best thing that a person can engage in is referred to as the _____ of doing the best thing and ignoring the next best thing to be done.
   a. AAB
   b. ABN Amro
   c. A Random Walk Down Wall Street
   d. Opportunity Cost

3. _____ are expenses that change in proportion to the activity of a business. In other words, _____ are the sum of marginal costs. It can also be considered normal costs. Along with fixed costs, _____ make up the two components of total cost. Direct Costs, however, are costs that can be associated with a particular cost object.
   a. Transaction cost
   b. Cost accounting
   c. Variable costs
   d. Fixed costs

4. _____ are costs that are not directly accountable to a particular function or product. _____ may be either fixed or variable. _____ include taxes, administration, personnel and security costs, and are also known as overhead.
   a. Indirect costs
   b. AAB
   c. Equivalent annual cost
   d. A Random Walk Down Wall Street

5. Accrual, in accounting, describes the accounting method known as _____, whereby revenues and expenses are recognized when they are accrued, i.e. accumulated (earned or incurred), regardless when the actual cash is received or paid out.

E.g. a company delivers a product to a customer who will pay for it 30 days later in the next fiscal year starting a week after the delivery. The company recognizes the proceeds as a revenue in its current income statement still for the fiscal year of the delivery, even though it will get paid in cash during the following accounting period.

a. Accrual basis
b. A Random Walk Down Wall Street
c. ABN Amro
d. AAB

6. _____ are business expenses that are not dependent on the level of production or sales. They tend to be time-related, such as salaries or rents being paid per month. This is in contrast to Variable costs, which are volume-related (and are paid per quantity.)

a. Fixed costs
b. Marginal cost
c. Transaction cost
d. Sliding scale fees

7. In economics and finance, _____ is the change in total cost that arises when the quantity produced changes by one unit. It is the cost of producing one more unit of a good. Mathematically, the _____ function is expressed as the first derivative of the total cost (TC) function with respect to quantity (Q). Note that the _____ may change with volume, and so at each level of production, the _____ is the cost of the next unit produced.

A typical _____ Curve

a. Marginal cost
b. Sliding scale fees
c. Fixed costs
d. Cost accounting

8. _____ is subcontracting a process, such as product design or manufacturing, to a third-party company. The decision to outsource is often made in the interest of lowering cost or making better use of time and energy costs, redirecting or conserving energy directed at the competencies of a particular business, or to make more efficient use of land, labor, capital, (information) technology and resources. _____ became part of the business lexicon during the 1980s.

a. OTC Bulletin Board
b. Exchange Rate Mechanism
c. AT'T Inc.
d. Outsourcing

9. In economics and business, specifically cost accounting, the _____ is the point at which cost or expenses and revenue are equal: there is no net loss or gain, and one has 'broken even'. A profit or a loss has not been made, although opportunity costs have been paid, and capital has received the risk-adjusted, expected return.

For example, if the business sells less than 200 tables each month, it will make a loss, if it sells more, it will be a profit.

a. Market microstructure
b. Break-even point
c. Fixed asset turnover
d. Defined contribution plan

10. In cost-volume-profit analysis, a form of management accounting, _____ is the marginal profit per unit sale. It is a useful quantity in carrying out various calculations, and can be used as a measure of operating leverage.

The Total _____ is Total Revenue (TR, or Sales) minus Total Variable Cost (TVC):

TContribution margin = TR >− TVC

The Unit _____ (C) is Unit Revenue (Price, P) minus Unit Variable Cost (V):

C = P >− V

The _____ Ratio is the percentage of Contribution over Total Revenue, which can be calculated from the unit contribution over unit price or total contribution over Total Revenue:

For instance, if the price is $10 and the unit variable cost is $2, then the unit _____ is $8, and the _____ ratio is $8/$10 = 80%.

a. 529 plan
b. 4-4-5 Calendar
c. 7-Eleven
d. Contribution margin

11. In finance, a _____ is collateral that the holder of a position in securities, options, or futures contracts has to deposit to cover the credit risk of his counterparty (most often his broker.) This risk can arise if the holder has done any of the following:

- borrowed cash from the counterparty to buy securities or options,
- sold securities or options short, or
- entered into a futures contract.

The collateral can be in the form of cash or securities, and it is deposited in a _____ account. On U.S. futures exchanges, '_____' was formally called performance bond.

_____ buying is buying securities with cash borrowed from a broker, using other securities as collateral.

a. Procter ' Gamble
b. Share
c. Credit
d. Margin

12. _____ is a costing model that identifies activities in an organization and assigns the cost of each activity resource to all products and services according to the actual consumption by each: it assigns more indirect costs (overhead) into direct costs.

In this way an organization can establish the true cost of its individual products and services for the purposes of identifying and eliminating those which are unprofitable and lowering the prices of those which are overpriced.

In a business organization, the ABC methodology assigns an organization's resource costs through activities to the products and services provided to its customers.

a. AAB
b. Indirect costs
c. Activity-based costing
d. A Random Walk Down Wall Street

Chapter 4. Understanding Costs

13. The phrase _____ refers to the aspect of corporate strategy, corporate finance and management dealing with the buying, selling and combining of different companies that can aid, finance, or help a growing company in a given industry grow rapidly without having to create another business entity.

An acquisition, also known as a takeover, is the buying of one company (the 'target') by another. An acquisition may be friendly or hostile.

a. 529 plan
b. 7-Eleven
c. 4-4-5 Calendar
d. Mergers and acquisitions

14. In business and accounting, _____s are everything of value that is owned by a person or company. The balance sheet of a firm records the monetary value of the _____s owned by the firm. The two major _____ classes are tangible _____s and intangible _____s.

a. EBITDA
b. Asset
c. Income
d. Accounts payable

Chapter 5. Capital Budgeting and Long-Term Financing

1. _____ is the planning process used to determine whether a firm's long term investments such as new machinery, replacement machinery, new plants, new products, and research development projects are worth pursuing. It is budget for major capital, or investment, expenditures.

Many formal methods are used in _____, including the techniques such as

- Net present value
- Profitability index
- Internal rate of return
- Modified Internal Rate of Return
- Equivalent annuity

These methods use the incremental cash flows from each potential investment, or project. Techniques based on accounting earnings and accounting rules are sometimes used - though economists consider this to be improper - such as the accounting rate of return, and 'return on investment.' Simplified and hybrid methods are used as well, such as payback period and discounted payback period.

a. Capital budgeting
b. Shareholder value
c. Financial distress
d. Preferred stock

2. In finance, the value of an option consists of two components, its intrinsic value and its _____. Time value is simply the difference between option value and intrinsic value. _____ is also known as theta, extrinsic value, or instrumental value.
   a. Global Squeeze
   b. Conservatism
   c. Time value
   d. Debt buyer

3. Simply put, _____ is the value of money figuring in a given amount of interest for a given amount of time. For example 100 dollars of todays money held for a year at 5 percent interest is worth 105 dollars, therefore 100 dollars paid now or 105 dollars paid exactly one year from now is the same amount of payment of money with that given intersest at that given amount of time. This notion dates at least to Martín de Azpilcueta of the School of Salamanca.

All of the standard calculations for _____ derive from the most basic algebraic expression for the present value of a future sum, 'discounted' to the present by an amount equal to the _____. For example, a sum of FV to be received in one year is discounted (at the rate of interest r) to give a sum of PV at present: PV = FV -- rÂ·PV = FV/(1+r).

Chapter 5. Capital Budgeting and Long-Term Financing

a. Zero-coupon bond
b. Coefficient of variation
c. Current account
d. Time value of money

4. _____ or financing is to provide capital (funds), which means money for a project, a person, a business or any other private or public institutions.

Those funds can be allocated for either short term or long term purposes. The health fund is a new way of _____ private healthcare centers.

a. Proxy fight
b. Funding
c. Synthetic CDO
d. Product life cycle

5. In economic models, the _____ time frame assumes no fixed factors of production. Firms can enter or leave the marketplace, and the cost (and availability) of land, labor, raw materials, and capital goods can be assumed to vary. In contrast, in the short-run time frame, certain factors are assumed to be fixed, because there is not sufficient time for them to change.

a. 529 plan
b. Short-run
c. Long-run
d. 4-4-5 Calendar

6. The phrase _____ refers to the aspect of corporate strategy, corporate finance and management dealing with the buying, selling and combining of different companies that can aid, finance, or help a growing company in a given industry grow rapidly without having to create another business entity.

An acquisition, also known as a takeover, is the buying of one company (the 'target') by another. An acquisition may be friendly or hostile.

a. Mergers and acquisitions
b. 7-Eleven
c. 529 plan
d. 4-4-5 Calendar

Chapter 5. Capital Budgeting and Long-Term Financing

7. _____ is the process of decreasing an amount over a period of time. The word comes from Middle English amortisen to kill, alienate in mortmain, from Anglo-French amorteser, alteration of amortir, from Vulgar Latin admortire to kill, from Latin ad- + mort-, mors death. Particular instances of the term include:

- _____ (business), the allocation of a lump sum amount to different time periods, particularly for loans and other forms of finance, including related interest or other finance charges.
    - _____ schedule, a table detailing each periodic payment on a loan (typically a mortgage), as generated by an _____ calculator.
    - Negative _____, an _____ schedule where the loan amount actually increases through not paying the full interest
- Amortized analysis, analyzing the execution cost of algorithms over a sequence of operations.
- _____ of capital expenditures of certain assets under accounting rules, particularly intangible assets, in a manner analogous to depreciation.
- _____ (tax law)

_____ is also used in the context of zoning regulations and describes the time in which a property owner has to relocate when the property's use constitutes a preexisting nonconforming use under zoning regulations.

- Depreciation

a. Intrinsic value
b. Option
c. AT'T Inc.
d. Amortization

8. _____ is a term used in accounting, economics and finance to spread the cost of an asset over the span of several years.

In simple words we can say that _____ is the reduction in the value of an asset due to usage, passage of time, wear and tear, technological outdating or obsolescence, depletion or other such factors.

In accounting, _____ is a term used to describe any method of attributing the historical or purchase cost of an asset across its useful life, roughly corresponding to normal wear and tear.

a. Bottom line
b. Matching principle
c. Deferred financing costs
d. Depreciation

Chapter 5. Capital Budgeting and Long-Term Financing

9. _____ refers to any one of several methods by which a company, for 'financial accounting' and/or tax purposes, depreciates a fixed asset in such a way that the amount of depreciation taken each year is higher during the earlier years of an asset's life. For financial accounting purposes, _____ is generally used when an asset is expected to be much more productive during its early years, so that depreciation expense will more accurately represent how much of an asset's usefulness is being used up each year. For tax purposes, _____ provides a way of deferring corporate income taxes by reducing taxable income in current years, in exchange for increased taxable income in future years.
   a. A Random Walk Down Wall Street
   b. Accelerated Depreciation
   c. ABN Amro
   d. AAB

10. In business and accounting, _____s are everything of value that is owned by a person or company. The balance sheet of a firm records the monetary value of the _____s owned by the firm. The two major _____ classes are tangible _____s and intangible _____s.
    a. Income
    b. EBITDA
    c. Accounts payable
    d. Asset

11. The term _____ has three unrelated technical definitions, and is also used in a variety of non-technical ways.

    - In financial economics, it refers to any asset used to make money, as opposed to assets used for personal enjoyment or consumption. This is an important distinction because two people can disagree sharply about the value of personal assets, one person might think a sports car is more valuable than a pickup truck, another person might have the opposite taste. But if an asset is held for the purpose of making money, taste has nothing to do with it, only differences of opinion about how much money the asset will produce. With the further assumption that people agree on the probability distribution of future cash flows, it is possible to have an objective _____ pricing model. Even without the assumption of agreement, it is possible to set rational limits on _____ value.
    - In governmental accounting, it is defined as any asset used in operations with an initial useful life extending beyond one reporting period. Generally, government managers have a 'stewardship' duty to maintain _____s under their control. See International Public Sector Accounting Standards for details.
    - In US tax accounting, it is defined as any property other than a list of exceptions. The main exceptions are anything held for sale, and any real estate or depreciable property used in business. Almost everything you own and use for personal purposes, pleasure or investment is a _____. If something is a _____ for tax purposes, gains or losses on sale or disposition are capital gains or capital losses. For individuals, however, capital losses on property held for personal use are generally not deductible. See the IRS publication Tax Facts about Capital Gains and Losses for details.

A well-known financial accounting textbook advises that the term be avoided except in tax accounting because it is used in so many different senses, not all of them well-defined. For example it is often used as a synonym for fixed assets or for investments in securities.

Chapter 5. Capital Budgeting and Long-Term Financing

A common non-technical usage occurs when people ask that employees or the environment or something else be treated as a _____.

a. Political risk
b. Settlement date
c. Solvency
d. Capital asset

12. In economics, business, and accounting, a _____ is the value of money that has been used up to produce something, and hence is not available for use anymore. In business, the _____ may be one of acquisition, in which case the amount of money expended to acquire it is counted as _____. In this case, money is the input that is gone in order to acquire the thing.

a. Fixed costs
b. Marginal cost
c. Sliding scale fees
d. Cost

13. _____ or economic opportunity loss is the value of the next best alternative foregone as the result of making a decision. _____ analysis is an important part of a company's decision-making processes but is not treated as an actual cost in any financial statement. The next best thing that a person can engage in is referred to as the _____ of doing the best thing and ignoring the next best thing to be done.

a. Opportunity cost
b. A Random Walk Down Wall Street
c. ABN Amro
d. AAB

14. _____ are costs incurred on the purchase of land, buildings, construction and equipment to be used in the production of goods or the rendering of services. In other words, the total cost needed to bring a project to a commercially operable status. However, _____ are not limited to the initial construction of a factory or other business.

a. Trade-off
b. Capital costs
c. Defined contribution plan
d. Capital outflow

15. The _____ is an expected return that the provider of capital plans to earn on their investment.

Chapter 5. Capital Budgeting and Long-Term Financing

Capital (money) used for funding a business should earn returns for the capital providers who risk their capital. For an investment to be worthwhile, the expected return on capital must be greater than the _____.

   a. Cost of Capital
   b. 4-4-5 Calendar
   c. Capital intensity
   d. Weighted average cost of capital

16. _____ is the concept of adding accumulated interest back to the principal, so that interest is earned on interest from that moment on. The act of declaring interest to be principal is called compounding (i.e., interest is compounded.) A loan, for example, may have its interest compounded every month: in this case, a loan with $100 principal and 1% interest per month would have a balance of $101 at the end of the first month.
   a. Risk management
   b. 4-4-5 Calendar
   c. Penny stock
   d. Compound interest

17. A '_____' is a 'Charge' that is paid to obtain the right to delay a payment. Essentially, the payer purchases the right to make a given payment in the future instead of in the Present. The '_____', or 'Charge' that must be paid to delay the payment, is simply the difference between what the payment amount would be if it were paid in the present and what the payment amount would be paid if it were paid in the future.
   a. Risk modeling
   b. Discount
   c. Risk aversion
   d. Value at risk

18. _____ is a fee paid on borrowed assets. It is the price paid for the use of borrowed money , or, money earned by deposited funds . Assets that are sometimes lent with _____ include money, shares, consumer goods through hire purchase, major assets such as aircraft, and even entire factories in finance lease arrangements.
   a. Insolvency
   b. A Random Walk Down Wall Street
   c. AAB
   d. Interest

19. _____ measures the nominal future sum of money that a given sum of money is 'worth' at a specified time in the future assuming a certain interest rate rate of return; it is the present value multiplied by the accumulation function.

The value does not include corrections for inflation or other factors that affect the true value of money in the future. This is used in time value of money calculations.

a. Present value of costs
b. Future value
c. Discounted cash flow
d. Future-oriented

20. _____ is the value on a given date of a future payment or series of future payments, discounted to reflect the time value of money and other factors such as investment risk. _____ calculations are widely used in business and economics to provide a means to compare cash flows at different times on a meaningful 'like to like' basis.

The most commonly applied model of the time value of money is compound interest.

a. Present value of benefits
b. Negative gearing
c. Net present value
d. Present value

21. An _____ can be defined as a contract which provides an income stream in return for an initial payment.

An immediate _____ is an _____ for which the time between the contract date and the date of the first payment is not longer than the time interval between payments. A common use for an immediate _____ is to provide a pension to a retired person or persons.

a. AT'T Inc.
b. Amortization
c. Intrinsic value
d. Annuity

Chapter 5. Capital Budgeting and Long-Term Financing

22. _____ is the balance of the amounts of cash being received and paid by a business during a defined period of time, sometimes tied to a specific project. Measurement of _____ can be used

- to evaluate the state or performance of a business or project.
- to determine problems with liquidity. Being profitable does not necessarily mean being liquid. A company can fail because of a shortage of cash, even while profitable.
- to generate project rate of returns. The time of _____s into and out of projects are used as inputs to financial models such as internal rate of return, and net present value.
- to examine income or growth of a business when it is believed that accrual accounting concepts do not represent economic realities. Alternately, _____ can be used to 'validate' the net income generated by accrual accounting.

_____ as a generic term may be used differently depending on context, and certain _____ definitions may be adapted by analysts and users for their own uses. Common terms include operating _____ and free _____.

_____s can be classified into:

1. Operational _____s: Cash received or expended as a result of the company's core business activities.
2. Investment _____s: Cash received or expended through capital expenditure, investments or acquisitions.
3. Financing _____s: Cash received or expended as a result of financial activities, such as interests and dividends.

All three together - the net _____ - are necessary to reconcile the beginning cash balance to the ending cash balance. Loan draw downs or equity injections, that is just shifting of capital but no expenditure as such, are not considered in the net _____.

a. Cash flow
b. Real option
c. Corporate finance
d. Shareholder value

23. In finance, the _____ approach describes a method of valuing a project, company, or asset using the concepts of the time value of money. All future cash flows are estimated and discounted to give their present values. The discount rate used is generally the appropriate cost of capital and may incorporate judgments of the uncertainty (riskiness) of the future cash flows.
   a. Present value of benefits
   b. Future-oriented
   c. Net present value
   d. Discounted cash flow

Chapter 5. Capital Budgeting and Long-Term Financing

24. The _____ is a capital budgeting metric used by firms to decide whether they should make investments. It is an indicator of the efficiency or quality of an investment, as opposed to net present value (NPV), which indicates value or magnitude.

The IRR is the annualized effective compounded return rate which can be earned on the invested capital, i.e., the yield on the investment.

   a. ABN Amro
   b. AAB
   c. A Random Walk Down Wall Street
   d. Internal rate of return

25. _____ or net present worth (NPW) is defined as the total present value (PV) of a time series of cash flows. It is a standard method for using the time value of money to appraise long-term projects. Used for capital budgeting, and widely throughout economics, it measures the excess or shortfall of cash flows, in present value terms, once financing charges are met.
   a. Net present value
   b. Negative gearing
   c. Tax shield
   d. Present value of costs

26. In finance, _____, also known as return on investment is the ratio of money gained or lost on an investment relative to the amount of money invested. The amount of money gained or lost may be referred to as interest, profit/loss, gain/loss, or net income/loss. The money invested may be referred to as the asset, capital, principal, or the cost basis of the investment.
   a. Doctrine of the Proper Law
   b. Composiition of Creditors
   c. Stock or scrip dividends
   d. Rate of return

27. The _____ is the rate of return that must be met for a company to undertake a particular project. The _____ is usually determined by evaluating existing opportunities in operations expansion, rate of return for investments, and other factors deemed relevant by management. A risk premium can also be attached to the _____ if management feels that specific opportunities inherently contain more risk than others that could be pursued with the same resources.
   a. Capital structure
   b. Corporate finance
   c. Gross profit
   d. Hurdle rate

Chapter 5. Capital Budgeting and Long-Term Financing

28. The _____ is an interest rate a central bank charges depository institutions that borrow reserves from it.

The term _____ has two meanings:

- the same as interest rate; the term 'discount' does not refer to the meaning of the word, but to the purpose of using the quantity, such as computations of present value, e.g. net present value / discounted cash flow

- the annual effective _____, which is the annual interest divided by the capital including that interest; this rate is lower than the interest rate; it corresponds to using the value after a year as the nominal value, and seeing the initial value as the nominal value minus a discount; it is used for Treasury Bills and similar financial instruments

The annual effective _____ is the annual interest divided by the capital including that interest, which is the interest rate divided by 100% plus the interest rate. It is the annual discount factor to be applied to the future cash flow, to find the discount, subtracted from a future value to find the value one year earlier.

For example, suppose there is a government bond that sells for $95 and pays $100 in a year's time.

  a. Stochastic volatility
  b. Black-Scholes
  c. Fisher equation
  d. Discount rate

29. _____ is that which is owed; usually referencing assets owed, but the term can cover other obligations. In the case of assets, _____ is a means of using future purchasing power in the present before a summation has been earned. Some companies and corporations use _____ as a part of their overall corporate finance strategy.
  a. Cross-collateralization
  b. Credit cycle
  c. Partial Payment
  d. Debt

30. In economics, the concept of the _____ refers to the decision-making time frame of a firm in which at least one factor of production is fixed. Costs which are fixed in the _____ have no impact on a firms decisions. For example a firm can raise output by increasing the amount of labour through overtime.
  a. 529 plan
  b. Short-run
  c. Long-run
  d. 4-4-5 Calendar

Chapter 5. Capital Budgeting and Long-Term Financing

31. _____ is the capital that a business raises by taking out a loan. It is a loan made to a company that is normally repaid at some future date. _____ differs from equity or share capital because subscribers to _____ do not become part owners of the business, but are merely creditors, and the suppliers of _____ usually receive a contractually fixed annual percentage return on their loan, and this is known as the coupon rate.

   a. Floating charge
   b. Financial assistance
   c. Risk-return spectrum
   d. Debt Capital

32. In finance, a _____ is a debt security, in which the authorized issuer owes the holders a debt and, depending on the terms of the _____, is obliged to pay interest (the coupon) and/or to repay the principal at a later date, termed maturity.

   Thus a _____ is a loan: the issuer is the borrower, the _____ holder is the lender, and the coupon is the interest. _____s provide the borrower with external funds to finance long-term investments, or, in the case of government _____s, to finance current expenditure.

   a. Bond
   b. Convertible bond
   c. Catastrophe bonds
   d. Puttable bond

33. _____ is a life of security. It may also refer to the final payment date of a loan or other financial instrument, at which point all remaining interest and principal is due to be paid.

   1, 3, 6 months _____ band can be calculated by using 30-day per month periods.

   a. False billing
   b. Maturity
   c. Primary market
   d. Replacement cost

34. _____ is the provision of resources (such as granting a loan) by one party to another party where that second party does not reimburse the first party immediately, thereby generating a debt, and instead arranges either to repay or return those resources (or material(s) of equal value) at a later date. The first party is called a creditor, also known as a lender, while the second party is called a debtor, also known as a borrower.

   Movements of financial capital are normally dependent on either _____ or equity transfers.

a. Comparable
b. Warrant
c. Clearing house
d. Credit

35. _____, refers to consumption opportunity gained by an entity within a specified time frame, which is generally expressed in monetary terms. However, for households and individuals, '_____ is the sum of all the wages, salaries, profits, interests payments, rents and other forms of earnings received... in a given period of time.' For firms, _____ generally refers to net-profit: what remains of revenue after expenses have been subtracted.
   a. Income
   b. Annual report
   c. OIBDA
   d. Accrual

36. A _____ is a document that indicates that the bearer of the document has title to property, such as shares or bonds. They differ from normal registered instruments, in that no records are kept of who owns the underlying property, or of the transactions involving transfer of ownership. Whoever physically holds the bearer bond papers owns the property.
   a. Marketable
   b. Bearer instrument
   c. Book entry
   d. Securities lending

37. A _____ is different from normal stock in that it is unregistered - no records are kept of the owner, or the transactions involving ownership. Whoever physically holds the _____ papers owns the stock or corporation. This is useful for investors and corporate officers who wish to retain anonymity.
   a. Clean price
   b. Revenue bonds
   c. Gilts
   d. Bearer bond

38. _____s are financial bonds that mature in installments over a period of time. In effect, a $100,000, 5-year _____ would mature in a $20,000 annuity over a 5-year interval. Bond issues consisting of a series of blocks of securities maturing in sequence, the coupon rate can be different.

a. Brady bonds
b. Bond fund
c. Callable bond
d. Serial bond

39. The coupon or _____ of a bond is the amount of interest paid per year expressed as a percentage of the face value of the bond.

For example if you hold $10,000 nominal of a bond described as a 4.5% loan stock, you will receive $450 in interest each year (probably in two installments of $225 each.)

Not all bonds have coupons.

a. Puttable bond
b. Zero-coupon bond
c. Coupon rate
d. Revenue bonds

40. A _____ is a bond bought at a price lower than its face value, with the face value repaid at the time of maturity. It does not make periodic interest payments, or so-called 'coupons,' hence the term zero-coupon bond. Investors earn return from the compounded interest all paid at maturity plus the difference between the discounted price of the bond and its par value.
a. Municipal bond
b. Bowie bonds
c. Callable bond
d. Zero coupon Bond

41. A _____ is a fund established by a government agency or business for the purpose of reducing debt.

The _____ was first used in Great Britain in the 18th century to reduce national debt. While used by Robert Walpole in 1716 and effectively in the 1720s and early 1730s, it originated in the commercial tax syndicates of the Italian peninsula of the 14th century to retire redeemable public debt of those cities.

a. Sinking fund
b. Modern portfolio theory
c. Debtor
d. Security interest

Chapter 5. Capital Budgeting and Long-Term Financing

42. An _____ is the price a borrower pays for the use of money they do not own, and the return a lender receives for deferring the use of funds, by lending it to the borrower. _____s are normally expressed as a percentage rate over the period of one year.

_____s targets are also a vital tool of monetary policy and are used to control variables like investment, inflation, and unemployment.

a. AAB
b. ABN Amro
c. Interest rate
d. A Random Walk Down Wall Street

43. _____ is a legal term for a type of debt which is overdue after missing an expected payment. It is also used (in the form in _____) for payments that occur at the end of a period.

_____ accrue from the date on the first missed payment was due.

a. Interest
b. Arrears
c. AAB
d. A Random Walk Down Wall Street

44. _____ is a process by which a firm can obtain the use of a certain fixed assets for which it must pay a series of contractual, periodic, tax deductable payments. The lessee is the receiver of the services or the assets under the lease contract and the lessor is the owner of the assets. The relationship between the tenant and the landlord is called a tenancy, and can be for a fixed or an indefinite period of time (called the term of the lease).

a. Quiet period
b. Foreign Corrupt Practices Act
c. Royalties
d. Leasing

45. In finance, 'participation' is an ownership interest in a mortgage or other loan. In particular, _____ is a cooperation of multiple lenders to issue a loan (known as participation loan) to one borrower. This is usually done in order to reduce individual risks of the lenders.

a. Short positions
b. Loan participation
c. Doctrine of the Proper Law
d. Securitization

46. _____ is the level of inventory that minimizes the total inventory holding costs and ordering costs. The framework used to determine this order quantity is also known as Wilson _____ Model. The model was developed by F. W. Harris in 1913.
   a. Economic order quantity
   b. AAB
   c. ABN Amro
   d. A Random Walk Down Wall Street

Chapter 6. Managing Short-Term Resources and Obligations

1. In accounting, a _____ is an asset on the balance sheet which is expected to be sold or otherwise used up in the near future, usually within one year, or one business cycle - whichever is longer. Typical _____s include cash, cash equivalents, accounts receivable, inventory, the portion of prepaid accounts which will be used within a year, and short-term investments.

On the balance sheet, assets will typically be classified into _____s and long-term assets.

   a. Historical cost
   b. Current asset
   c. Write-off
   d. Long-term liabilities

2. In economics, the concept of the _____ refers to the decision-making time frame of a firm in which at least one factor of production is fixed. Costs which are fixed in the _____ have no impact on a firms decisions. For example a firm can raise output by increasing the amount of labour through overtime.
   a. 4-4-5 Calendar
   b. 529 plan
   c. Long-run
   d. Short-run

3. In business and accounting, _____s are everything of value that is owned by a person or company. The balance sheet of a firm records the monetary value of the _____s owned by the firm. The two major _____ classes are tangible _____s and intangible _____s.
   a. EBITDA
   b. Accounts payable
   c. Asset
   d. Income

4. In accounting, _____ are considered liabilities of the business that are to be settled in cash within the fiscal year or the operating cycle, whichever period is longer.

For example accounts payable for goods, services or supplies that were purchased for use in the operation of the business and payable within a normal period of time would be _____.

Bonds, mortgages and loans that are payable over a term exceeding one year would be fixed liabilities.

a. Net income
b. Gross sales
c. Current liabilities
d. Closing entries

5. In the most general sense, a _____ is anything that is a hindrance, or puts individuals at a disadvantage.

Before we discuss the financial terms, we should note that a _____ can also have a much more important slang meaning.

This is best described in an example.

a. Liability
b. McFadden Act
c. Limited liability
d. Covenant

6. _____ is a financial metric which represents operating liquidity available to a business. Along with fixed assets such as plant and equipment, _____ is considered a part of operating capital. It is calculated as current assets minus current liabilities.
a. Working capital management
b. 4-4-5 Calendar
c. 529 plan
d. Working capital

7. Decisions relating to working capital and short term financing are referred to as _____. These involve managing the relationship between a firm's short-term assets and its short-term liabilities. The goal of _____ is to ensure that the firm is able to continue its operations and that it has sufficient cash flow to satisfy both maturing short-term debt and upcoming operational expenses.
a. Working capital
b. 4-4-5 Calendar
c. 529 plan
d. Working capital management

8. _____ are securities that can be easily converted into cash. Such securities will generally have highly liquid markets allowing the security to be sold at a reasonable price very quickly. This is a usual feature in real estate .

Chapter 6. Managing Short-Term Resources and Obligations

a. Book entry
b. Marketable
c. Tracking stock
d. Securities lending

9. A _____ is a fungible, negotiable instrument representing financial value. They are broadly categorized into debt securities (such as banknotes, bonds and debentures), and equity securities; e.g., common stocks. The company or other entity issuing the _____ is called the issuer.

a. Book entry
b. Securities lending
c. Security
d. Tracking stock

10. A _____ s a time deposit, a financial product commonly offered to consumers by banks, thrift institutions, and credit unions.

They are similar to savings accounts in that they are insured and thus virtually risk-free; they are 'money in the bank'. They are different from savings accounts in that they have a specific, fixed term (often three months, six months, or one to five years), and, usually, a fixed interest rate.

a. Variable rate mortgage
b. Reserve requirement
c. Time deposit
d. Certificate of deposit

11. The free _____ of a public company is an estimate of the proportion of shares that are not held by large owners and that are not stock with sales restrictions (restricted stock that cannot be sold until they become unrestricted stock.)

The free _____ or a public _____ is usually defined as being all shares held by investors other than:

- shares held by owners owning more than 5% of all shares (those could be institutional investors, 'strategic shareholders,' founders, executives, and other insiders' holdings)
- restricted stocks (granted to executives that can be, but don't have to be, registered insiders)
- insider holdings (it is assumed that insiders hold stock for the very long term)

The free _____ is an important criterion in quoting a share on the stock market.

Chapter 6. Managing Short-Term Resources and Obligations

To _____ a company means to list its shares on a public stock exchange through an initial public offering (or 'flotation'.)

- Open market
- Outstanding shares
- Market capitalization
- Public _____ *loat*
- Reverse takeover

a. Synthetic CDO
b. Trade finance
c. Golden parachute
d. Float

12. Accrual, in accounting, describes the accounting method known as _____, whereby revenues and expenses are recognized when they are accrued, i.e. accumulated (earned or incurred), regardless when the actual cash is received or paid out.

E.g. a company delivers a product to a customer who will pay for it 30 days later in the next fiscal year starting a week after the delivery. The company recognizes the proceeds as a revenue in its current income statement still for the fiscal year of the delivery, even though it will get paid in cash during the following accounting period.

a. ABN Amro
b. A Random Walk Down Wall Street
c. Accrual basis
d. AAB

13. Working capital requirements of a business should be monitored at all times to ensure that there are sufficient funds available to meet short-term expenses.

The _____ is basically a detailed plan that shows all expected sources and uses of cash

a. Rate of return
b. Mitigating Control
c. Loans and interest, in Judaism
d. Cash budget

Chapter 6. Managing Short-Term Resources and Obligations 47

14. A _____ is any credit facility extended to a business by a bank or financial institution. A _____ may take several forms such as cash credit, overdraft, demand loan, export packing credit, term loan, discounting or purchase of commercial bills etc. It is like an account that can readily be tapped into if the need arises or not touched at all and saved for emergencies.
    a. Cash credit
    b. Default Notice
    c. Debt-snowball method
    d. Line of credit

15. _____, in bookkeeping, refers to assets, liabilities, income, and expenses recorded on individual pages of the so called book of final entry or ledger. Changes in _____ value are made by chronologically posting debit (DR) and credit (CR) entries to its page. Examples of _____s are cash, _____s receivable, mortgages, loans, land and buildings, common stock, sales, services provided, wages, and payroll overhead.
    a. Alpha
    b. Option
    c. Accretion
    d. Account

16. _____ is the provision of resources (such as granting a loan) by one party to another party where that second party does not reimburse the first party immediately, thereby generating a debt, and instead arranges either to repay or return those resources (or material(s) of equal value) at a later date. The first party is called a creditor, also known as a lender, while the second party is called a debtor, also known as a borrower.

Movements of financial capital are normally dependent on either _____ or equity transfers.

    a. Clearing house
    b. Warrant
    c. Comparable
    d. Credit

17. _____ is that which is owed; usually referencing assets owed, but the term can cover other obligations. In the case of assets, _____ is a means of using future purchasing power in the present before a summation has been earned. Some companies and corporations use _____ as a part of their overall corporate finance strategy.
    a. Partial Payment
    b. Cross-collateralization
    c. Credit cycle
    d. Debt

Chapter 6. Managing Short-Term Resources and Obligations

18. _____ is the level of inventory that minimizes the total inventory holding costs and ordering costs. The framework used to determine this order quantity is also known as Wilson _____ Model. The model was developed by F. W. Harris in 1913.

   a. ABN Amro
   b. A Random Walk Down Wall Street
   c. AAB
   d. Economic order quantity

19. In finance, the _____ is the global financial market for short-term borrowing and lending. It provides short-term liquidity funding for the global financial system. The _____ is where short-term obligations such as Treasury bills, commercial paper and bankers' acceptances are bought and sold.

   a. Debt-for-equity swap
   b. Cramdown
   c. Consumer debt
   d. Money market

20. _____ mature in one year or less. Like zero-coupon bonds, they do not pay interest prior to maturity; instead they are sold at a discount of the par value to create a positive yield to maturity. Many regard _____ as the least risky investment available to U.S. investors.

   a. Treasury bills
   b. 4-4-5 Calendar
   c. Treasury securities
   d. Treasury Inflation Protected Securities

21. In the global money market, _____ is an unsecured promissory note with a fixed maturity of one to 270 days. _____ is a money-market security issued (sold) by large banks and corporations to get money to meet short term debt obligations (for example, payroll), and is only backed by an issuing bank or corporation's promise to pay the face amount on the maturity date specified on the note. Since it is not backed by collateral, only firms with excellent credit ratings from a recognized rating agency will be able to sell their _____ at a reasonable price.

   a. Commercial paper
   b. Trade-off theory
   c. Book building
   d. Financial distress

22. A _____ is a financial contract whose value is derived from the value of something else (known as the underlying.) The underlying on which a _____ is based can be an asset, weather conditions bonds or other forms of credit.

Chapter 6. Managing Short-Term Resources and Obligations

a. 4-4-5 Calendar
b. Derivative
c. 7-Eleven
d. 529 plan

23. A _____ allows a borrower to use a financial security as collateral for a cash loan at a fixed rate of interest. In a repo, the borrower agrees to immediately sell a security to a lender and also agrees to buy the same security from the lender at a fixed price at some later date. A repo is equivalent to a cash transaction combined with a forward contract.

   a. Volatility arbitrage
   b. Total return swap
   c. Contango
   d. Repurchase agreement

24. _____ is one of a series of accounting transactions dealing with the billing of customers who owe money to a person, company or organization for goods and services that have been provided to the customer. In most business entities this is typically done by generating an invoice and mailing or electronically delivering it to the customer, who in turn must pay it within an established timeframe called credit or payment terms.

An example of a common payment term is Net 30, meaning payment is due in the amount of the invoice 30 days from the date of invoice.

   a. Income
   b. Impaired asset
   c. Accounting methods
   d. Accounts receivable

25. In accounting and finance, _____ is the portion of receivables that can no longer be collected, typically from accounts receivable or loans. _____ in accounting is considered an expense.

There are two methods to account for _____:

   1. Direct write off method (Non - GAAP)

A receivable which is not considered collectible is charged directly to the income statement.

   1. Allowance method (GAAP)

An estimate is made at the end of each fiscal year of the amount of _____. This is then accumulated in a provision which is then used to reduce specific receivable accounts as and when necessary.

a. Bad debt
b. 4-4-5 Calendar
c. 529 plan
d. Tax expense

26. _____ is a list for goods and materials held available in stock by a business. It is also used for a list of the contents of a household and for a list for testamentary purposes of the possessions of someone who has died. In accounting _____ is considered an asset.
   a. Inventory
   b. ABN Amro
   c. A Random Walk Down Wall Street
   d. AAB

27. In marketing, _____ refers to the total cost of holding inventory. This includes warehousing costs such as rent, utilities and salaries, financial costs such as opportunity cost, and inventory costs related to perishibility, shrinkage and insurance.
   a. 529 plan
   b. 7-Eleven
   c. 4-4-5 Calendar
   d. Carrying cost

28. In economics, business, and accounting, a _____ is the value of money that has been used up to produce something, and hence is not available for use anymore. In business, the _____ may be one of acquisition, in which case the amount of money expended to acquire it is counted as _____. In this case, money is the input that is gone in order to acquire the thing.
   a. Marginal cost
   b. Fixed costs
   c. Sliding scale fees
   d. Cost

29. _____ is an inventory strategy implemented to improve the return on investment of a business by reducing in-process inventory and its associated carrying costs. In order to achieve _____ the process must have signals of what is going on elsewhere within the process. This means that the process is often driven by a series of signals, which can be Kanban, that tell production processes when to make the next part.

Chapter 6. Managing Short-Term Resources and Obligations

a. Just-in-time
b. Debtor-in-possession financing
c. Pac-Man defense
d. Greed and fear

30. _____ is a file or account that contains money that a person or company owes to suppliers, but hasn't paid yet (a form of debt.) When you receive an invoice you add it to the file, and then you remove it when you pay. Thus, the A/P is a form of credit that suppliers offer to their purchasers by allowing them to pay for a product or service after it has already been received.

a. Accrual
b. Earnings before interest, taxes, depreciation and amortization
c. Outstanding balance
d. Accounts payable

31. In a company, _____ is the sum of all financial records of salaries, wages, bonuses and deductions.

A paycheck, is traditionally a paper document issued by an employer to pay an employee for services rendered. While most commonly used in the United States, recently the physical paycheck has been increasingly replaced by electronic direct deposit to bank accounts.

a. 529 plan
b. 4-4-5 Calendar
c. Tax expense
d. Payroll

32. _____ exists when one firm provides goods or services to a customer with an agreement to bill them later, or receive a shipment or service from a supplier under an agreement to pay them later. It can be viewed as an essential element of capitalization in an operating business because it can reduce the required capital investment to operate the business if it is managed properly. _____ is the largest use of capital for a majority of business to business (B2B) sellers in the United States and is a critical source of capital for a majority of all businesses.

a. Trade credit
b. 529 plan
c. Going concern
d. 4-4-5 Calendar

33. In finance, a _____ is a debt security, in which the authorized issuer owes the holders a debt and, depending on the terms of the _____, is obliged to pay interest (the coupon) and/or to repay the principal at a later date, termed maturity.

Thus a _____ is a loan: the issuer is the borrower, the _____ holder is the lender, and the coupon is the interest. _____s provide the borrower with external funds to finance long-term investments, or, in the case of government _____s, to finance current expenditure.

a. Catastrophe bonds
b. Convertible bond
c. Puttable bond
d. Bond

34. In lending agreements, _____ is a borrower's pledge of specific property to a lender, to secure repayment of a loan. The _____ serves as protection for a lender against a borrower's risk of default - that is, a borrower failing to pay the principal and interest under the terms of a loan obligation. If a borrower does default on a loan (due to insolvency or other event), that borrower forfeits (gives up) the property pledged as _____ *ollateral* - and the lender then becomes the owner of the _____.

a. Nominal value
b. Future-oriented
c. Refinancing risk
d. Collateral

Chapter 7. Accountability and Control

1. In accounting and organizational theory, _____ is defined as a process effected by an organization's structure, work and authority flows, people and management information systems, designed to help the organization accomplish specific goals or objectives. It is a means by which an organization's resources are directed, monitored, and measured. It plays an important role in preventing and detecting fraud and protecting the organization's resources, both physical (e.g., machinery and property) and intangible (e.g., reputation or intellectual property such as trademarks.)
    a. Asian Financial Crisis
    b. Internal control
    c. OTC Bulletin Board
    d. Interest

2. The _____ of 2002 (Pub.L. 107-204, 116 Stat. 745, enacted July 30, 2002), also known as the Public Company Accounting Reform and Investor Protection Act of 2002 and commonly called Sarbanes-Oxley, Sarbox or SOX, is a United States federal law enacted on July 30, 2002 in response to a number of major corporate and accounting scandals including those affecting Enron, Tyco International, Adelphia, Peregrine Systems and WorldCom.
    a. Sarbanes-Oxley Act
    b. Foreign Corrupt Practices Act
    c. Duty of loyalty
    d. Blue sky law

3. In probability theory and statistics, the _____ of a random variable, probability distribution averaging the squared distance of its possible values from the expected value (mean.) Whereas the mean is a way to describe the location of a distribution, the _____ is a way to capture its scale or degree of being spread out. The unit of _____ is the square of the unit of the original variable.
    a. Harmonic mean
    b. Monte Carlo methods
    c. Semivariance
    d. Variance

4. In business, _____ is income that a company receives from its normal business activities, usually from the sale of goods and services to customers. Some companies also receive _____ from interest, dividends or royalties paid to them by other companies. _____ may refer to business income in general, or it may refer to the amount, in a monetary unit, received during a period of time, as in 'Last year, Company X had _____ of $32 million.'

In many countries, including the UK, _____ is referred to as turnover.

   a. Bottom line
   b. Furniture, Fixtures and Equipment
   c. Matching principle
   d. Revenue

Chapter 7. Accountability and Control

5. In economics, business, and accounting, a _____ is the value of money that has been used up to produce something, and hence is not available for use anymore. In business, the _____ may be one of acquisition, in which case the amount of money expended to acquire it is counted as _____. In this case, money is the input that is gone in order to acquire the thing.

   a. Fixed costs
   b. Sliding scale fees
   c. Marginal cost
   d. Cost

6. _____ are expenses that change in proportion to the activity of a business. In other words, _____ are the sum of marginal costs. It can also be considered normal costs. Along with fixed costs, _____ make up the two components of total cost. Direct Costs, however, are costs that can be associated with a particular cost object.

   a. Cost accounting
   b. Fixed costs
   c. Variable costs
   d. Transaction cost

7. _____ or audit log is a chronological sequence of audit records, each of which contains evidence directly pertaining to and resulting from the execution of a business process or system function.

   Audit records typically result from activities such as transactions or communications by individual people, systems, accounts or other entities.

   Webopedia defines an _____ as 'a record showing who has accessed a computer system and what operations he or she has performed during a given period of time.' ()

   In telecommunication, the term means a record of both completed and attempted accesses and service, or data forming a logical path linking a sequence of events, used to trace the transactions that have affected the contents of a record.

   a. AAB
   b. ABN Amro
   c. A Random Walk Down Wall Street
   d. Audit trail

8. The role of the _____ is to issue accounting standards in the United Kingdom. It is recognised for that purpose under the Companies Act 1985. It took over the task of setting accounting standards from the Accounting Standards Committee (ASC) in 1990.

a. ABN Amro
b. AAB
c. A Random Walk Down Wall Street
d. Accounting Standards Board

9. _____ measures the nominal future sum of money that a given sum of money is 'worth' at a specified time in the future assuming a certain interest rate rate of return; it is the present value multiplied by the accumulation function.

The value does not include corrections for inflation or other factors that affect the true value of money in the future. This is used in time value of money calculations.

a. Discounted cash flow
b. Future-oriented
c. Present value of costs
d. Future value

10. _____ is the standard framework of guidelines for financial accounting used in the United States of America. It includes the standards, conventions, and rules accountants follow in recording and summarizing transactions, and in the preparation of financial statements. _____ are now issued by the Financial Accounting Standards Board (FASB).

a. Revenue
b. Net income
c. Depreciation
d. Generally Accepted Accounting Principles

11. The _____ is currently the source of generally accepted accounting principles (GAAP) used by State and Local governments in the United States of America. As with most of the entities involved in creating GAAP in the United States, it is a private, non-governmental organization.

The _____ is subject to oversight by the Financial Accounting Foundation (FAF), which selects the members of the _____ and the Financial Accounting Standards Board, and funds both organizations.

a. General partnership
b. Wells Fargo ' Co.
c. Depository Trust Company
d. Governmental Accounting Standards Board

12. The _____ is one of the measures of national income and input for a given country's economy. _____ is defined as the total cost of all finished goods and services produced within the country in a stipulated period of time (usually a 365-day year.) It is sometimes regarded as the sum of profits added at every level of production (the intermediate stages) of all final goods and services produced within a country in a stipulated timeframe, and it is rarely given a monetary value.
   a. Recession
   b. Macroeconomics
   c. Behavioral finance
   d. Gross domestic product

13. _____ is an umbrella term which refers to the various accounting systems used by various public sector entities. In the United States, for instance, there are three levels of government which follow different accounting standards set forth by independent, private sector boards. At the federal level, the Federal Accounting Standards Advisory Board (FASAB) sets forth the accounting standards to follow.
   a. Governmental Accounting
   b. Grenzplankostenrechnung
   c. Nonassurance services
   d. Management accounting

14. _____ refers to an examination of a program, function, operation or the management systems and procedures of a governmental or non-profit entity to assess whether the entity is achieving economy, efficiency and effectiveness in the employment of available resources. The examination is objective and systematic, generally using structured and professionally adopted methodologies.

In most countries, _____s of governmental activities are carried out by the external audit bodies at federal or state level.

   a. Generally Accepted Auditing Standards
   b. Trustworthy Repositories Audit ' Certification
   c. Performance audit
   d. Clinical audit

Chapter 8. Taking Stock of Where You Are: The Balance Sheet

1. In financial accounting, a _____ or statement of financial position is a summary of a person's or organization's balances. Assets, liabilities and ownership equity are listed as of a specific date, such as the end of its financial year. A _____ is often described as a snapshot of a company's financial condition.
   a. Balance sheet
   b. Financial statements
   c. Statement on Auditing Standards No. 70: Service Organizations
   d. Statement of retained earnings

2. _____ is the field of accountancy concerned with the preparation of financial statements for decision makers, such as stockholders, suppliers, banks, employees, government agencies, owners, and other stakeholders. The fundamental need for _____ is to reduce principal-agent problem by measuring and monitoring agents' performance and reporting the results to interested users.

   _____ is used to prepare accounting information for people outside the organization or not involved in the day to day running of the company.

   a. 7-Eleven
   b. Financial accounting
   c. 4-4-5 Calendar
   d. 529 plan

3. _____ is the standard framework of guidelines for financial accounting used in the United States of America. It includes the standards, conventions, and rules accountants follow in recording and summarizing transactions, and in the preparation of financial statements. _____ are now issued by the Financial Accounting Standards Board (FASB).
   a. Revenue
   b. Net income
   c. Depreciation
   d. Generally Accepted Accounting Principles

4. _____ is concerned with the provisions and use of accounting information to managers within organizations, to provide them with the basis to make informed business decisions that will allow them to be better equipped in their management and control functions.

   In contrast to financial accountancy information, _____ information is:

   - usually confidential and used by management, instead of publicly reported;
   - forward-looking, instead of historical;
   - pragmatically computed using extensive management information systems and internal controls, instead of complying with accounting standards.

58 *Chapter 8. Taking Stock of Where You Are: The Balance Sheet*

This is because of the different emphasis: _____ information is used within an organization, typically for decision-making.

According to the Chartered Institute of Management Accountants, _____ is 'the process of identification, measurement, accumulation, analysis, preparation, interpretation and communication of information used by management to plan, evaluate and control within an entity and to assure appropriate use of and accountability for its Resource (economics)resources. _____ also comprises the preparation of financial reports for non-management groups such as shareholders, creditors, regulatory agencies and tax authorities'.

   a. Governmental accounting
   b. Nonassurance services
   c. Management accounting
   d. Grenzplankostenrechnung

5. _____ is the level of inventory that minimizes the total inventory holding costs and ordering costs. The framework used to determine this order quantity is also known as Wilson _____ Model. The model was developed by F. W. Harris in 1913.
   a. AAB
   b. A Random Walk Down Wall Street
   c. ABN Amro
   d. Economic order quantity

6. In the most general sense, a _____ is anything that is a hindrance, or puts individuals at a disadvantage.

Before we discuss the financial terms, we should note that a _____ can also have a much more important slang meaning.

This is best described in an example.

   a. McFadden Act
   b. Covenant
   c. Limited liability
   d. Liability

7. _____ are sometimes the same as net worth, or shareholders' equity - assets minus liabilities. The term _____ is commonly used with charities or not for profit entities. Although these entities don't make money, it is important to maintain reasonable reserves to help future growth.

Chapter 8. Taking Stock of Where You Are: The Balance Sheet

a. Sustainable growth rate
b. Cash conversion cycle
c. Sharpe ratio
d. Net assets

8. In business, _____ is the total assets minus total outside liabilities of an individual or a company. For a company, this is called shareholders' equity and may be referred to as book value. _____ is stated as at a particular point in time.
   a. Restructuring
   b. Moneylender
   c. Certified International Investment Analyst
   d. Net worth

9. In business and accounting, _____s are everything of value that is owned by a person or company. The balance sheet of a firm records the monetary value of the _____s owned by the firm. The two major _____ classes are tangible _____s and intangible _____s.
   a. Income
   b. Accounts payable
   c. EBITDA
   d. Asset

10. _____, in bookkeeping, refers to assets, liabilities, income, and expenses recorded on individual pages of the so called book of final entry or ledger. Changes in _____ value are made by chronologically posting debit (DR) and credit (CR) entries to its page. Examples of _____s are cash, _____s receivable, mortgages, loans, land and buildings, common stock, sales, services provided, wages, and payroll overhead.
    a. Accretion
    b. Account
    c. Option
    d. Alpha

11. _____ is one of a series of accounting transactions dealing with the billing of customers who owe money to a person, company or organization for goods and services that have been provided to the customer. In most business entities this is typically done by generating an invoice and mailing or electronically delivering it to the customer, who in turn must pay it within an established timeframe called credit or payment terms.

An example of a common payment term is Net 30, meaning payment is due in the amount of the invoice 30 days from the date of invoice.

a. Impaired asset
b. Accounting methods
c. Income
d. Accounts receivable

12. _____ are defined as identifiable non-monetary assets that cannot be seen, touched or physically measured, which are created through time and/or effort and that are identifiable as a separate asset. There are two primary forms of intangibles - legal intangibles (such as trade secrets (e.g., customer lists), copyrights, patents, trademarks, and goodwill) and competitive intangibles (such as knowledge activities (know-how, knowledge), collaboration activities, leverage activities, and structural activities.) Legal intangibles generate legal property rights defensible in a court of law.
a. ABN Amro
b. A Random Walk Down Wall Street
c. AAB
d. Intangible assets

13. A _____ is a party (e.g. person, organization, company, or government) that has a claim to the services of a second party. The first party, in general, has provided some property or service to the second party under the assumption (usually enforced by contract) that the second party will return an equivalent property or service. The second party is frequently called a debtor or borrower.
a. Redemption value
b. False billing
c. Creditor
d. NOPLAT

14. _____ is an accounting term used to reflect the portion of the book value of a business entity not directly attributable to its assets and liabilities; it normally arises only in case of an acquisition. It reflects the ability of the entity to make a higher profit than would be derived from selling the tangible assets. _____ is also known as an intangible asset.
a. Net profit
b. Consolidation
c. Cost of goods sold
d. Goodwill

15. _____ is a file or account that contains money that a person or company owes to suppliers, but hasn't paid yet (a form of debt.) When you receive an invoice you add it to the file, and then you remove it when you pay. Thus, the A/P is a form of credit that suppliers offer to their purchasers by allowing them to pay for a product or service after it has already been received.

a. Outstanding balance
b. Accrual
c. Earnings before interest, taxes, depreciation and amortization
d. Accounts payable

16. In lending agreements, _____ is a borrower's pledge of specific property to a lender, to secure repayment of a loan. The _____ serves as protection for a lender against a borrower's risk of default - that is, a borrower failing to pay the principal and interest under the terms of a loan obligation. If a borrower does default on a loan (due to insolvency or other event), that borrower forfeits (gives up) the property pledged as _____ _ollateral_ - and the lender then becomes the owner of the _____.
a. Nominal value
b. Future-oriented
c. Refinancing risk
d. Collateral

17. In accounting the separate _____ treats a business as distinct and completely separate from the owners. The business stands apart from other organizations as separate economic unit. It is necessary to record the business transactions separately to distinguish it from the owner's personal transactions. This concept is now extended to accounting for various divisions of a firm in order to ascertain results for each division.
a. Imprest system
b. Unified Ledger Accounting
c. Installment Sales Method
d. Entity concept

18. In economics, business, and accounting, a _____ is the value of money that has been used up to produce something, and hence is not available for use anymore. In business, the _____ may be one of acquisition, in which case the amount of money expended to acquire it is counted as _____. In this case, money is the input that is gone in order to acquire the thing.
a. Fixed costs
b. Sliding scale fees
c. Marginal cost
d. Cost

19. In business, investment, and accounting, the principle or convention of _____ has at least two meanings.

In investment and finance, it is a strategy which aims at long-term capital appreciation with low risk. It can be characterized as moderate or cautious and is the opposite of aggressive behavior.

Chapter 8. Taking Stock of Where You Are: The Balance Sheet

a. Duration gap
b. Barcampbank
c. Conservatism
d. Debt-snowball method

20. _____ is a term used in accounting, economics and finance to spread the cost of an asset over the span of several years.

In simple words we can say that _____ is the reduction in the value of an asset due to usage, passage of time, wear and tear, technological outdating or obsolescence, depletion or other such factors.

In accounting, _____ is a term used to describe any method of attributing the historical or purchase cost of an asset across its useful life, roughly corresponding to normal wear and tear.

a. Deferred financing costs
b. Depreciation
c. Matching principle
d. Bottom line

21. A _____ is a business that functions without the intention or threat of liquidation for the foreseeable future, usually regarded as at least within 12 months.

In accounting, '_____' refers to a company's ability to continue functioning as a business entity. It is the responsibility of the directors to assess whether the _____ assumption is appropriate when preparing the financial statements.

a. Trade credit
b. 529 plan
c. 4-4-5 Calendar
d. Going concern

22. _____ is a concept or convention within auditing and accounting relating to the importance of an amount, transaction, or discrepancy. The objective of an audit of financial statements is to enable the auditor to express an opinion whether the financial statements are prepared, in all material respects, in conformity with an identified financial reporting framework such as Generally Accepted Accounting Principles (GAAP.) The assessment of what is material is a matter of professional judgment.

Chapter 8. Taking Stock of Where You Are: The Balance Sheet

a. Clinical audit
b. Financial audit
c. Trustworthy Repositories Audit ' Certification
d. Materiality

23. Accrual, in accounting, describes the accounting method known as _____, whereby revenues and expenses are recognized when they are accrued, i.e. accumulated (earned or incurred), regardless when the actual cash is received or paid out.

E.g. a company delivers a product to a customer who will pay for it 30 days later in the next fiscal year starting a week after the delivery. The company recognizes the proceeds as a revenue in its current income statement still for the fiscal year of the delivery, even though it will get paid in cash during the following accounting period.

a. Accrual basis
b. AAB
c. ABN Amro
d. A Random Walk Down Wall Street

24. Two primary accounting methods, _____ and accrual basis, are used to calculate taxable income for U.S. federal income taxes. According to the Internal Revenue Code, a taxpayer may compute taxable income by:

1. the Cash receipts and disbursements method;
2. an accrual method;
3. any other method permitted by the chapter; or
4. any combination of the foregoing methods permitted under regulations prescribed by the Secretary.

As a general rule, a taxpayer must compute taxable income using the same accounting method he uses to compute income in keeping his books. Also, the taxpayer must maintain a consistent method of accounting from year to year. Should he change from the _____ to the accrual basis (or vice versa), he must notify and secure the consent of the Secretary.

a. Cash basis
b. 529 plan
c. 4-4-5 Calendar
d. 7-Eleven

25. A _____ (or financial year, or sometimes budget year) is a period used for calculating annual ('yearly') financial statements in businesses and other organizations. In many jurisdictions, regulatory laws regarding accounting and taxation require such reports once per twelve months, but do not require that the period reported on constitutes a calendar year (i.e., January through December.) _____s vary between businesses and countries.

a. Fiscal year
b. Purchase ledger
c. Special journals
d. Matching principle

26. In accounting, a _____ is an asset on the balance sheet which is expected to be sold or otherwise used up in the near future, usually within one year, or one business cycle - whichever is longer. Typical _____s include cash, cash equivalents, accounts receivable, inventory, the portion of prepaid accounts which will be used within a year, and short-term investments.

On the balance sheet, assets will typically be classified into _____s and long-term assets.

a. Historical cost
b. Current asset
c. Long-term liabilities
d. Write-off

27. In accounting, _____ are considered liabilities of the business that are to be settled in cash within the fiscal year or the operating cycle, whichever period is longer.

For example accounts payable for goods, services or supplies that were purchased for use in the operation of the business and payable within a normal period of time would be _____.

Bonds, mortgages and loans that are payable over a term exceeding one year would be fixed liabilities.

a. Closing entries
b. Gross sales
c. Net income
d. Current liabilities

28. _____ plant, and equipment, is a term used in accountancy for assets and property which cannot easily be converted into cash. This can be compared with current assets such as cash or bank accounts, which are described as liquid assets. In most cases, only tangible assets are referred to as fixed.

a. Percentage of Completion
b. Remittance advice
c. Petty cash
d. Fixed asset

Chapter 8. Taking Stock of Where You Are: The Balance Sheet   65

29. In economic models, the _____ time frame assumes no fixed factors of production. Firms can enter or leave the marketplace, and the cost (and availability) of land, labor, raw materials, and capital goods can be assumed to vary. In contrast, in the short-run time frame, certain factors are assumed to be fixed, because there is not sufficient time for them to change.
   a. 4-4-5 Calendar
   b. 529 plan
   c. Short-run
   d. Long-run

30. In economics, the concept of the _____ refers to the decision-making time frame of a firm in which at least one factor of production is fixed. Costs which are fixed in the _____ have no impact on a firms decisions. For example a firm can raise output by increasing the amount of labour through overtime.
   a. Short-run
   b. 529 plan
   c. Long-run
   d. 4-4-5 Calendar

31. Cash and _____ are the most liquid assets found within the asset portion of a company's balance sheet. _____ are assets that are readily convertible into cash, such as money market holdings, short-term government bonds or Treasury bills, marketable securities and commercial paper. _____ are distinguished from other investments through their short-term existence; they mature within 3 months whereas short-term investments are 12 months or less, and long-term investments are any investments that mature in excess of 12 months.
   a. Par value
   b. Tick size
   c. Secured debt
   d. Cash equivalents

32. In accounting and finance, _____ is the portion of receivables that can no longer be collected, typically from accounts receivable or loans. _____ in accounting is considered an expense.

There are two methods to account for _____:

   1. Direct write off method (Non - GAAP)

A receivable which is not considered collectible is charged directly to the income statement.

   1. Allowance method (GAAP)

An estimate is made at the end of each fiscal year of the amount of _____. This is then accumulated in a provision which is then used to reduce specific receivable accounts as and when necessary.

Chapter 8. Taking Stock of Where You Are: The Balance Sheet

a. 4-4-5 Calendar
b. Tax expense
c. 529 plan
d. Bad debt

33. _____ is that which is owed; usually referencing assets owed, but the term can cover other obligations. In the case of assets, _____ is a means of using future purchasing power in the present before a summation has been earned. Some companies and corporations use _____ as a part of their overall corporate finance strategy.

a. Debt
b. Partial Payment
c. Credit cycle
d. Cross-collateralization

34. _____ are securities that can be easily converted into cash. Such securities will generally have highly liquid markets allowing the security to be sold at a reasonable price very quickly. This is a usual feature in real estate.

a. Book entry
b. Securities lending
c. Tracking stock
d. Marketable

35. A _____ is a fungible, negotiable instrument representing financial value. They are broadly categorized into debt securities (such as banknotes, bonds and debentures), and equity securities; e.g., common stocks. The company or other entity issuing the _____ is called the issuer.

a. Book entry
b. Security
c. Securities lending
d. Tracking stock

36. _____, in accrual accounting, is any account where the asset or liability is not realized until a future date, e.g. annuities, charges, taxes, income, etc. The _____ item may be carried, dependent on type of deferral, as either an asset or liability. See also: accrual

_____ is also used in the university admissions process. It is the action by which a school rejects a student for early admission but still opts to review that student in the general admissions pool.

Chapter 8. Taking Stock of Where You Are: The Balance Sheet

a. Revenue
b. Net profit
c. Deferred
d. Current asset

37. _____ is a list for goods and materials held available in stock by a business. It is also used for a list of the contents of a household and for a list for testamentary purposes of the possessions of someone who has died. In accounting _____ is considered an asset.

a. AAB
b. ABN Amro
c. A Random Walk Down Wall Street
d. Inventory

38. _____ is the process of decreasing an amount over a period of time. The word comes from Middle English amortisen to kill, alienate in mortmain, from Anglo-French amorteser, alteration of amortir, from Vulgar Latin admortire to kill, from Latin ad- + mort-, mors death. Particular instances of the term include:

- _____ (business), the allocation of a lump sum amount to different time periods, particularly for loans and other forms of finance, including related interest or other finance charges.
    - _____ schedule, a table detailing each periodic payment on a loan (typically a mortgage), as generated by an _____ calculator.
    - Negative _____, an _____ schedule where the loan amount actually increases through not paying the full interest
- Amortized analysis, analyzing the execution cost of algorithms over a sequence of operations.
- _____ of capital expenditures of certain assets under accounting rules, particularly intangible assets, in a manner analogous to depreciation.
- _____ (tax law)

_____ is also used in the context of zoning regulations and describes the time in which a property owner has to relocate when the property's use constitutes a preexisting nonconforming use under zoning regulations.

- Depreciation

a. Intrinsic value
b. Amortization
c. AT'T Inc.
d. Option

Chapter 8. Taking Stock of Where You Are: The Balance Sheet

39. In accounting, _____ or *Carrying value* is the value of an asset according to its balance sheet account balance. For assets, the value is based on the original cost of the asset less any depreciation, amortization or impairment costs made against the asset. A company's _____ is its total assets minus intangible assets and liabilities.

   a. Book value
   b. Pro forma
   c. Retained earnings
   d. Current liabilities

40. A _____ is a fund established by a government agency or business for the purpose of reducing debt.

The _____ was first used in Great Britain in the 18th century to reduce national debt. While used by Robert Walpole in 1716 and effectively in the 1720s and early 1730s, it originated in the commercial tax syndicates of the Italian peninsula of the 14th century to retire redeemable public debt of those cities.

   a. Modern portfolio theory
   b. Debtor
   c. Sinking fund
   d. Security interest

41. An _____ is a lease whose term is short compared to the useful life of the asset or piece of equipment (an airliner, a ship etc.) being leased. An _____ is commonly used to acquire equipment on a relatively short-term basis.

   a. ABN Amro
   b. AAB
   c. A Random Walk Down Wall Street
   d. Operating lease

42. The phrase _____ refers to the aspect of corporate strategy, corporate finance and management dealing with the buying, selling and combining of different companies that can aid, finance, or help a growing company in a given industry grow rapidly without having to create another business entity.

An acquisition, also known as a takeover, is the buying of one company (the 'target') by another. An acquisition may be friendly or hostile.

   a. 4-4-5 Calendar
   b. 7-Eleven
   c. 529 plan
   d. Mergers and acquisitions

Chapter 8. Taking Stock of Where You Are: The Balance Sheet

43. A finance lease or _____ is a type of lease. It is a commercial arrangement where:

- the lessee (customer or borrower) will select an asset (equipment, vehicle, software);
- the lessor (finance company) will purchase that asset;
- the lessee will have use of that asset during the lease;
- the lessee will pay a series of rentals or installments for the use of that asset;
- the lessor will recover a large part or all of the cost of the asset plus earn interest from the rentals paid by the lessee;
- the lessee has the option to acquire ownership of the asset (e.g. paying the last rental, or bargain option purchase price);

The finance company is the legal owner of the asset during duration of the lease.

However the lessee has control over the asset providing them the benefits and risks of (economic) ownership.

A finance lease differs from an operating lease in that:

- in a finance lease the lessee has use of the asset over most of its economic life and beyond (generally by making small 'peppercorn' payments at the end of the lease term.)

In an operating lease the lessee only uses the asset for some of the asset's life.

- in a finance lease the lessor will recover all or most of the cost of the equipment from the rentals paid by the lessee.

In an operating lease the lessor will have a substantial investment or residual value on completion of the lease.

- in a finance lease the lessee has the benefits and risks of economic ownership of the asset (e.g. risk of obsolescence, paying for maintenance, claiming capital allowances/depreciation.)

In an operating lease the lessor has the benefits and risks of owning the asset.

The U.S. Financial Accounting Standards Board and the International Accounting Standards Board announced in 2006 a joint project to comprehensively review lease accounting standards.

a. Capitalization rate
b. Cash management
c. Capital Lease
d. Cash concentration

44. In finance, a _____ is a debt security, in which the authorized issuer owes the holders a debt and, depending on the terms of the _____, is obliged to pay interest (the coupon) and/or to repay the principal at a later date, termed maturity.

Thus a _____ is a loan: the issuer is the borrower, the _____ holder is the lender, and the coupon is the interest. _____s provide the borrower with external funds to finance long-term investments, or, in the case of government _____s, to finance current expenditure.

   a. Convertible bond
   b. Puttable bond
   c. Bond
   d. Catastrophe bonds

45. _____ mature in one year or less. Like zero-coupon bonds, they do not pay interest prior to maturity; instead they are sold at a discount of the par value to create a positive yield to maturity. Many regard _____ as the least risky investment available to U.S. investors.
   a. Treasury bills
   b. 4-4-5 Calendar
   c. Treasury Inflation Protected Securities
   d. Treasury securities

46. The _____ is where double entry bookkeeping entries are recorded by debiting one account and crediting another account with the same amount. The amount debited and the amount credited should always be equal, thereby ensuring the accounting equation is maintained.

Depending on the business's accounting information system, specialized journals may be used in conjunction with the _____ for record-keeping.

   a. Journal entry
   b. General ledger
   c. Ledger
   d. General journal

47. The _____ is a capital budgeting metric used by firms to decide whether they should make investments. It is an indicator of the efficiency or quality of an investment, as opposed to net present value (NPV), which indicates value or magnitude.

The IRR is the annualized effective compounded return rate which can be earned on the invested capital, i.e., the yield on the investment.

Chapter 8. Taking Stock of Where You Are: The Balance Sheet

a. A Random Walk Down Wall Street
b. Internal rate of return
c. ABN Amro
d. AAB

48. A _____, in accounting, is a logging of transcriptions into items accounting journal. The _____ can consist of several items, each of which is either a debit or a credit. The total of the debits must equal the total of the credits, or the _____ is said to be 'unbalanced.' Journal entries can record unique items or recurring items such as depreciation or bond amortization.
    a. General ledger
    b. Ledger
    c. General journal
    d. Journal entry

49. _____ is an inventory strategy implemented to improve the return on investment of a business by reducing in-process inventory and its associated carrying costs. In order to achieve _____ the process must have signals of what is going on elsewhere within the process. This means that the process is often driven by a series of signals, which can be Kanban, that tell production processes when to make the next part.
    a. Debtor-in-possession financing
    b. Greed and fear
    c. Pac-Man defense
    d. Just-in-time

50. In finance, _____, also known as return on investment is the ratio of money gained or lost on an investment relative to the amount of money invested. The amount of money gained or lost may be referred to as interest, profit/loss, gain/loss, or net income/loss. The money invested may be referred to as the asset, capital, principal, or the cost basis of the investment.
    a. Composiition of Creditors
    b. Stock or scrip dividends
    c. Doctrine of the Proper Law
    d. Rate of return

51. _____ is the provision of resources (such as granting a loan) by one party to another party where that second party does not reimburse the first party immediately, thereby generating a debt, and instead arranges either to repay or return those resources (or material(s) of equal value) at a later date. The first party is called a creditor, also known as a lender, while the second party is called a debtor, also known as a borrower.

Movements of financial capital are normally dependent on either _____ or equity transfers.

Chapter 8. Taking Stock of Where You Are: The Balance Sheet

a. Warrant
b. Clearing house
c. Comparable
d. Credit

52. An _____ can be defined as a contract which provides an income stream in return for an initial payment.

An immediate _____ is an _____ for which the time between the contract date and the date of the first payment is not longer than the time interval between payments. A common use for an immediate _____ is to provide a pension to a retired person or persons.

a. Intrinsic value
b. AT'T Inc.
c. Amortization
d. Annuity

53. The _____, sometimes known as the nominal ledger, is the main accounting record of a business which uses double-entry bookkeeping. It will usually include accounts for such items as current assets, fixed assets, liabilities, revenue and expense items, gains and losses.

The _____ is a collection of the group of accounts that supports the items shown in the major financial statements.

a. Ledger
b. General ledger
c. General journal
d. Journal entry

54. A _____ is the principal book for recording transactions. Originally, the term referred to a large volume of Scripture/service book kept in one place in church and accessible.

According to Charles Wriothesley's Chronicle (1538):

> the curates should provide a booke of the bible in Englishe, of the largest volume, to be a lidger in the same church for the parishioners to read on.

It is an application of this original meaning that is found in the commercial usage of the term for the principal book of account in a business house, the general _____ or nominal _____ and also in the terms purchase _____ and sales _____.

a. Ledger
b. General ledger
c. Journal entry
d. General journal

55. A _____, in business matters, is an entity that is controlled by a bigger and more powerful entity. The controlled entity is called a company, corporation, or limited liability company, and the controlling entity is called its parent (or the parent company.) The reason for this distinction is that a lone company cannot be a _____ of any organization; only an entity representing a legal fiction as a separate entity can be a _____.
   a. Joint stock company
   b. 4-4-5 Calendar
   c. 529 plan
   d. Subsidiary

74   Chapter 9. Reporting the Results of Operations: The Activity and Cash Flow Statements

1. _____ is the balance of the amounts of cash being received and paid by a business during a defined period of time, sometimes tied to a specific project. Measurement of _____ can be used

- to evaluate the state or performance of a business or project.
- to determine problems with liquidity. Being profitable does not necessarily mean being liquid. A company can fail because of a shortage of cash, even while profitable.
- to generate project rate of returns. The time of _____s into and out of projects are used as inputs to financial models such as internal rate of return, and net present value.
- to examine income or growth of a business when it is believed that accrual accounting concepts do not represent economic realities. Alternately, _____ can be used to 'validate' the net income generated by accrual accounting.

_____ as a generic term may be used differently depending on context, and certain _____ definitions may be adapted by analysts and users for their own uses. Common terms include operating _____ and free _____.

_____s can be classified into:

1. Operational _____s: Cash received or expended as a result of the company's core business activities.
2. Investment _____s: Cash received or expended through capital expenditure, investments or acquisitions.
3. Financing _____s: Cash received or expended as a result of financial activities, such as interests and dividends.

All three together - the net _____ - are necessary to reconcile the beginning cash balance to the ending cash balance. Loan draw downs or equity injections, that is just shifting of capital but no expenditure as such, are not considered in the net _____.

a. Cash flow
b. Shareholder value
c. Real option
d. Corporate finance

2. In financial accounting, a _____ or statement of cash flows is a financial statement that shows a company's flow of cash. The money coming into the business is called cash inflow, and money going out from the business is called cash outflow. The statement shows how changes in balance sheet and income accounts affect cash and cash equivalents, and breaks the analysis down to operating, investing, and financing activities.
a. 529 plan
b. 4-4-5 Calendar
c. 7-Eleven
d. Cash flow statement

Chapter 9. Reporting the Results of Operations: The Activity and Cash Flow Statements 75

3. In business, _____ is income that a company receives from its normal business activities, usually from the sale of goods and services to customers. Some companies also receive _____ from interest, dividends or royalties paid to them by other companies. _____ may refer to business income in general, or it may refer to the amount, in a monetary unit, received during a period of time, as in 'Last year, Company X had _____ of $32 million.'

In many countries, including the UK, _____ is referred to as turnover.

   a. Furniture, Fixtures and Equipment
   b. Revenue
   c. Matching principle
   d. Bottom line

4. _____ is equal to the income that a firm has after subtracting costs and expenses from the total revenue. _____ can be distributed among holders of common stock as a dividend or held by the firm as retained earnings. _____ is an accounting term; in some countries (such as the UK) profit is the usual term.
   a. Write-off
   b. Historical cost
   c. Furniture, Fixtures and Equipment
   d. Net income

5. _____ is the difference between price and the costs of bringing to market whatever it is that is accounted as an enterprise (whether by harvest, extraction, manufacture, or purchase) in terms of the component costs of delivered goods and/or services and any operating or other expenses.

A key difficulty in measuring profit is in defining costs. Pure economic monetary profits can be zero or negative even in competitive equilibrium when accounted monetized costs exceed monetized price.

   a. Accounting profit
   b. Economic profit
   c. A Random Walk Down Wall Street
   d. AAB

6. _____, refers to consumption opportunity gained by an entity within a specified time frame, which is generally expressed in monetary terms. However, for households and individuals, '_____ is the sum of all the wages, salaries, profits, interests payments, rents and other forms of earnings received... in a given period of time.' For firms, _____ generally refers to net-profit: what remains of revenue after expenses have been subtracted.

76   Chapter 9. Reporting the Results of Operations: The Activity and Cash Flow Statements

a. Accrual
b. OIBDA
c. Income
d. Annual report

7. In economics, business, and accounting, a _____ is the value of money that has been used up to produce something, and hence is not available for use anymore. In business, the _____ may be one of acquisition, in which case the amount of money expended to acquire it is counted as _____. In this case, money is the input that is gone in order to acquire the thing.

a. Sliding scale fees
b. Fixed costs
c. Marginal cost
d. Cost

8. _____ is the standard framework of guidelines for financial accounting used in the United States of America. It includes the standards, conventions, and rules accountants follow in recording and summarizing transactions, and in the preparation of financial statements. _____ are now issued by the Financial Accounting Standards Board (FASB).

a. Revenue
b. Depreciation
c. Generally Accepted Accounting Principles
d. Net income

9. Accrual, in accounting, describes the accounting method known as _____, whereby revenues and expenses are recognized when they are accrued, i.e. accumulated (earned or incurred), regardless when the actual cash is received or paid out.

E.g. a company delivers a product to a customer who will pay for it 30 days later in the next fiscal year starting a week after the delivery. The company recognizes the proceeds as a revenue in its current income statement still for the fiscal year of the delivery, even though it will get paid in cash during the following accounting period.

a. AAB
b. ABN Amro
c. Accrual basis
d. A Random Walk Down Wall Street

10. In accounting and finance, _____ is the portion of receivables that can no longer be collected, typically from accounts receivable or loans. _____ in accounting is considered an expense.

Chapter 9. Reporting the Results of Operations: The Activity and Cash Flow Statements

There are two methods to account for _____:

1. Direct write off method (Non - GAAP)

A receivable which is not considered collectible is charged directly to the income statement.

1. Allowance method (GAAP)

An estimate is made at the end of each fiscal year of the amount of _____. This is then accumulated in a provision which is then used to reduce specific receivable accounts as and when necessary.

a. 4-4-5 Calendar
b. Tax expense
c. 529 plan
d. Bad debt

11. _____ is that which is owed; usually referencing assets owed, but the term can cover other obligations. In the case of assets, _____ is a means of using future purchasing power in the present before a summation has been earned. Some companies and corporations use _____ as a part of their overall corporate finance strategy.
a. Cross-collateralization
b. Partial Payment
c. Credit cycle
d. Debt

12. In business and accounting, _____s are everything of value that is owned by a person or company. The balance sheet of a firm records the monetary value of the _____s owned by the firm. The two major _____ classes are tangible _____s and intangible _____s.
a. Asset
b. Accounts payable
c. Income
d. EBITDA

13. _____ is a term used in accounting, economics and finance to spread the cost of an asset over the span of several years.

In simple words we can say that _____ is the reduction in the value of an asset due to usage, passage of time, wear and tear, technological outdating or obsolescence, depletion or other such factors.

Chapter 9. Reporting the Results of Operations: The Activity and Cash Flow Statements

In accounting, _____ is a term used to describe any method of attributing the historical or purchase cost of an asset across its useful life, roughly corresponding to normal wear and tear.

a. Bottom line
b. Matching principle
c. Deferred financing costs
d. Depreciation

14. Depreciation methods that provide for a higher depreciation charge in the first year of an asset's life and gradually decreasing charges in subsequent years are called accelerated depreciation methods. This may be a more realistic reflection of an asset's actual expected benefit from the use of the asset: many assets are most useful when they are new. One popular accelerated method is the declining-balance method. Under this method the Book Value is multiplied by a fixed rate.

The most common rate used is double the straight-line rate. For this reason, this technique is referred to as the _____. To illustrate, suppose a business has an asset with $1,000 Original Cost, $100 Salvage Value, and 5 years useful life. First, calculate straight-line depreciation rate. Since the asset has 5 years useful life, the straight-line depreciation rate equals (100% / 5) 20% per year. With _____, as the name suggests, double that rate, or 40% depreciation rate is used.

a. Doctrine of the Proper Law
b. Double-declining-balance method
c. The Goodyear Tire ' Rubber Company
d. Database auditing

15. _____ refers to any one of several methods by which a company, for 'financial accounting' and/or tax purposes, depreciates a fixed asset in such a way that the amount of depreciation taken each year is higher during the earlier years of an asset's life. For financial accounting purposes, _____ is generally used when an asset is expected to be much more productive during its early years, so that depreciation expense will more accurately represent how much of an asset's usefulness is being used up each year. For tax purposes, _____ provides a way of deferring corporate income taxes by reducing taxable income in current years, in exchange for increased taxable income in future years.

a. ABN Amro
b. AAB
c. A Random Walk Down Wall Street
d. Accelerated Depreciation

16. _____, in accrual accounting, is any account where the asset or liability is not realized until a future date, e.g. annuities, charges, taxes, income, etc. The _____ item may be carried, dependent on type of deferral, as either an asset or liability.See also: accrual

Chapter 9. Reporting the Results of Operations: The Activity and Cash Flow Statements 79

_____ is also used in the university admissions process. It is the action by which a school rejects a student for early admission but still opts to review that student in the general admissions pool.

a. Net profit
b. Revenue
c. Current asset
d. Deferred

17. _____ are the earnings returned on the initial investment amount.

In the US, the Financial Accounting Standards Board (FASB) requires companies' income statements to report _____ for each of the major categories of the income statement: continuing operations, discontinued operations, extraordinary items, and net income.

The _____ formula does not include preferred dividends for categories outside of continued operations and net income.

a. Average accounting return
b. Assets turnover
c. Inventory turnover
d. Earnings per share

18. In business and finance, a _____ (also referred to as equity _____) of stock means a _____ of ownership in a corporation (company.) In the plural, stocks is often used as a synonym for _____s especially in the United States, but it is less commonly used that way outside of North America.

In the United Kingdom, South Africa, and Australia, stock can also refer to completely different financial instruments such as government bonds or, less commonly, to all kinds of marketable securities.

a. Procter ' Gamble
b. Bucket shop
c. Margin
d. Share

19. _____ refers to an assessment of the viability, stability and profitability of a business, sub-business or project.

Chapter 9. Reporting the Results of Operations: The Activity and Cash Flow Statements

It is performed by professionals who prepare reports using ratios that make use of information taken from financial statements and other reports. These reports are usually presented to top management as one of their bases in making business decisions.

a. 4-4-5 Calendar
b. Value investing
c. Financial analysis
d. 529 plan

20. _____ is the process of decreasing an amount over a period of time. The word comes from Middle English amortisen to kill, alienate in mortmain, from Anglo-French amorteser, alteration of amortir, from Vulgar Latin admortire to kill, from Latin ad- + mort-, mors death. Particular instances of the term include:

- _____ (business), the allocation of a lump sum amount to different time periods, particularly for loans and other forms of finance, including related interest or other finance charges.
    - _____ schedule, a table detailing each periodic payment on a loan (typically a mortgage), as generated by an _____ calculator.
    - Negative _____, an _____ schedule where the loan amount actually increases through not paying the full interest
- Amortized analysis, analyzing the execution cost of algorithms over a sequence of operations.
- _____ of capital expenditures of certain assets under accounting rules, particularly intangible assets, in a manner analogous to depreciation.
- _____ (tax law)

_____ is also used in the context of zoning regulations and describes the time in which a property owner has to relocate when the property's use constitutes a preexisting nonconforming use under zoning regulations.

- Depreciation

a. Intrinsic value
b. AT'T Inc.
c. Option
d. Amortization

21. _____ are formal records of a business' financial activities.

Chapter 9. Reporting the Results of Operations: The Activity and Cash Flow Statements 81

_____ provide an overview of a business' financial condition in both short and long term. There are four basic _____:

1. **Balance sheet**: also referred to as statement of financial position or condition, reports on a company's assets, liabilities, and net equity as of a given point in time.
2. **Income statement**: also referred to as Profit and Loss statement (or a 'P'L'), reports on a company's income, expenses, and profits over a period of time.
3. **Statement of retained earnings**: explains the changes in a company's retained earnings over the reporting period.
4. **Statement of cash flows**: reports on a company's cash flow activities, particularly its operating, investing and financing activities.

a. Statement on Auditing Standards No. 70: Service Organizations
b. Notes to the Financial Statements
c. Statement of retained earnings
d. Financial statements

22. _____ is a list of all accounts including a unique number identifying each. A _____ can track a specific financial information. Each account in the chart has assigned a unique identifier, typically an account number.
   a. Journal entry
   b. General ledger
   c. General journal
   d. Chart of accounts

23. _____, in bookkeeping, refers to assets, liabilities, income, and expenses recorded on individual pages of the so called book of final entry or ledger. Changes in _____ value are made by chronologically posting debit (DR) and credit (CR) entries to its page. Examples of _____s are cash, _____s receivable, mortgages, loans, land and buildings, common stock, sales, services provided, wages, and payroll overhead.
   a. Alpha
   b. Accretion
   c. Option
   d. Account

24. The _____, sometimes known as the nominal ledger, is the main accounting record of a business which uses double-entry bookkeeping. It will usually include accounts for such items as current assets, fixed assets, liabilities, revenue and expense items, gains and losses.

Chapter 9. Reporting the Results of Operations: The Activity and Cash Flow Statements

The _____ is a collection of the group of accounts that supports the items shown in the major financial statements.

a. General ledger
b. Journal entry
c. Ledger
d. General journal

25. A _____ is the principal book for recording transactions. Originally, the term referred to a large volume of Scripture/service book kept in one place in church and accessible.

According to Charles Wriothesley's Chronicle (1538):

> the curates should provide a booke of the bible in Englishe, of the largest volume, to be a lidger in the same church for the parishioners to read on.

It is an application of this original meaning that is found in the commercial usage of the term for the principal book of account in a business house, the general _____ or nominal _____ and also in the terms purchase _____ and sales _____.

a. General journal
b. Ledger
c. Journal entry
d. General ledger

26. _____ is a list for goods and materials held available in stock by a business. It is also used for a list of the contents of a household and for a list for testamentary purposes of the possessions of someone who has died. In accounting _____ is considered an asset.

a. AAB
b. A Random Walk Down Wall Street
c. ABN Amro
d. Inventory

27. An _____ allows a company to provide a monetary value for items that make up their inventory. Inventories are usually the largest current asset of a business, and proper measurement of them is necessary to assure accurate financial statements. If inventory is not properly measured, expenses and revenues cannot be properly matched and a company could make poor business decisions.

a. AAB
b. ABN Amro
c. Inventory valuation
d. A Random Walk Down Wall Street

28. In finance, _____ is the process of estimating the potential market value of a financial asset or liability. they can be done on assets (for example, investments in marketable securities such as stocks, options, business enterprises, or intangible assets such as patents and trademarks) or on liabilities (e.g., Bonds issued by a company.) _____s are required in many contexts including investment analysis, capital budgeting, merger and acquisition transactions, financial reporting, taxable events to determine the proper tax liability, and in litigation.
   a. Valuation
   b. Share
   c. Procter ' Gamble
   d. Margin

Chapter 10. Unique Aspects of Accounting for Not-for-Profit and Health Care Organizations

1. _____ is the standard framework of guidelines for financial accounting used in the United States of America. It includes the standards, conventions, and rules accountants follow in recording and summarizing transactions, and in the preparation of financial statements. _____ are now issued by the Financial Accounting Standards Board (FASB).
    a. Depreciation
    b. Net income
    c. Revenue
    d. Generally Accepted Accounting Principles

2. In financial accounting, a _____ or statement of financial position is a summary of a person's or organization's balances. Assets, liabilities and ownership equity are listed as of a specific date, such as the end of its financial year. A _____ is often described as a snapshot of a company's financial condition.
    a. Balance Sheet
    b. Statement on Auditing Standards No. 70: Service Organizations
    c. Financial statements
    d. Statement of retained earnings

3. _____ are formal records of a business' financial activities.

   _____ provide an overview of a business' financial condition in both short and long term. There are four basic _____:

    1. **Balance sheet**: also referred to as statement of financial position or condition, reports on a company's assets, liabilities, and net equity as of a given point in time.
    2. **Income statement**: also referred to as Profit and Loss statement (or a 'P'L'), reports on a company's income, expenses, and profits over a period of time.
    3. **Statement of retained earnings**: explains the changes in a company's retained earnings over the reporting period.
    4. **Statement of cash flows**: reports on a company's cash flow activities, particularly its operating, investing and financing activities.

    a. Statement on Auditing Standards No. 70: Service Organizations
    b. Statement of retained earnings
    c. Notes to the Financial Statements
    d. Financial statements

4. _____ is an accounting system often used by nonprofit organizations and by the public sector.

   _____ serves any nonprofit organization or the public sector. These organizations have a need for special reporting to financial statements users that show how money is spent, rather than how much profit was earned.

Chapter 10. Unique Aspects of Accounting for Not-for-Profit and Health Care Organizations

a. False billing
b. Death spiral financing
c. Bonus share
d. Fund Accounting

5. _____ are sometimes the same as net worth, or shareholders' equity - assets minus liabilities. The term _____ is commonly used with charities or not for profit entities. Although these entities don't make money, it is important to maintain reasonable reserves to help future growth.
   a. Cash conversion cycle
   b. Sharpe ratio
   c. Net assets
   d. Sustainable growth rate

6. _____ mature in one year or less. Like zero-coupon bonds, they do not pay interest prior to maturity; instead they are sold at a discount of the par value to create a positive yield to maturity. Many regard _____ as the least risky investment available to U.S. investors.
   a. Treasury securities
   b. Treasury Inflation Protected Securities
   c. 4-4-5 Calendar
   d. Treasury bills

7. In business and accounting, _____s are everything of value that is owned by a person or company. The balance sheet of a firm records the monetary value of the _____s owned by the firm. The two major _____ classes are tangible _____s and intangible _____s.
   a. Income
   b. Accounts payable
   c. EBITDA
   d. Asset

Chapter 10. Unique Aspects of Accounting for Not-for-Profit and Health Care Organizations

8. _____ is the balance of the amounts of cash being received and paid by a business during a defined period of time, sometimes tied to a specific project. Measurement of _____ can be used

- to evaluate the state or performance of a business or project.
- to determine problems with liquidity. Being profitable does not necessarily mean being liquid. A company can fail because of a shortage of cash, even while profitable.
- to generate project rate of returns. The time of _____s into and out of projects are used as inputs to financial models such as internal rate of return, and net present value.
- to examine income or growth of a business when it is believed that accrual accounting concepts do not represent economic realities. Alternately, _____ can be used to 'validate' the net income generated by accrual accounting.

_____ as a generic term may be used differently depending on context, and certain _____ definitions may be adapted by analysts and users for their own uses. Common terms include operating _____ and free _____.

_____s can be classified into:

1. Operational _____s: Cash received or expended as a result of the company's core business activities.
2. Investment _____s: Cash received or expended through capital expenditure, investments or acquisitions.
3. Financing _____s: Cash received or expended as a result of financial activities, such as interests and dividends.

All three together - the net _____ - are necessary to reconcile the beginning cash balance to the ending cash balance. Loan draw downs or equity injections, that is just shifting of capital but no expenditure as such, are not considered in the net _____.

a. Shareholder value
b. Real option
c. Cash flow
d. Corporate finance

9. In business, _____ is income that a company receives from its normal business activities, usually from the sale of goods and services to customers. Some companies also receive _____ from interest, dividends or royalties paid to them by other companies. _____ may refer to business income in general, or it may refer to the amount, in a monetary unit, received during a period of time, as in 'Last year, Company X had _____ of $32 million.'

In many countries, including the UK, _____ is referred to as turnover.

a. Bottom line
b. Furniture, Fixtures and Equipment
c. Revenue
d. Matching principle

10. In economic models, the _____ time frame assumes no fixed factors of production. Firms can enter or leave the marketplace, and the cost (and availability) of land, labor, raw materials, and capital goods can be assumed to vary. In contrast, in the short-run time frame, certain factors are assumed to be fixed, because there is not sufficient time for them to change.

a. 4-4-5 Calendar
b. Short-run
c. 529 plan
d. Long-run

11. _____ is a term used in accounting, economics and finance to spread the cost of an asset over the span of several years.

In simple words we can say that _____ is the reduction in the value of an asset due to usage, passage of time, wear and tear, technological outdating or obsolescence, depletion or other such factors.

In accounting, _____ is a term used to describe any method of attributing the historical or purchase cost of an asset across its useful life, roughly corresponding to normal wear and tear.

a. Matching principle
b. Deferred financing costs
c. Bottom line
d. Depreciation

12. _____ is a life of security. It may also refer to the final payment date of a loan or other financial instrument, at which point all remaining interest and principal is due to be paid.

1, 3, 6 months _____ band can be calculated by using 30-day per month periods.

a. Replacement cost
b. False billing
c. Primary market
d. Maturity

Chapter 10. Unique Aspects of Accounting for Not-for-Profit and Health Care Organizations

13. A _____ is a fungible, negotiable instrument representing financial value. They are broadly categorized into debt securities (such as banknotes, bonds and debentures), and equity securities; e.g., common stocks. The company or other entity issuing the _____ is called the issuer.

   a. Securities lending
   b. Security
   c. Book entry
   d. Tracking stock

14. _____ is that which is owed; usually referencing assets owed, but the term can cover other obligations. In the case of assets, _____ is a means of using future purchasing power in the present before a summation has been earned. Some companies and corporations use _____ as a part of their overall corporate finance strategy.

   a. Partial Payment
   b. Credit cycle
   c. Cross-collateralization
   d. Debt

Chapter 11. Unique Aspects of Accounting for State and Local Governments

1. The role of the _____ is to issue accounting standards in the United Kingdom. It is recognised for that purpose under the Companies Act 1985. It took over the task of setting accounting standards from the Accounting Standards Committee (ASC) in 1990.

   a. A Random Walk Down Wall Street
   b. AAB
   c. ABN Amro
   d. Accounting Standards Board

2. _____ is the standard framework of guidelines for financial accounting used in the United States of America. It includes the standards, conventions, and rules accountants follow in recording and summarizing transactions, and in the preparation of financial statements. _____ are now issued by the Financial Accounting Standards Board (FASB).

   a. Net income
   b. Depreciation
   c. Revenue
   d. Generally Accepted Accounting Principles

3. _____ is an umbrella term which refers to the various accounting systems used by various public sector entities. In the United States, for instance, there are three levels of government which follow different accounting standards set forth by independent, private sector boards. At the federal level, the Federal Accounting Standards Advisory Board (FASAB) sets forth the accounting standards to follow.

   a. Nonassurance services
   b. Governmental Accounting
   c. Grenzplankostenrechnung
   d. Management accounting

4. The _____ is currently the source of generally accepted accounting principles (GAAP) used by State and Local governments in the United States of America. As with most of the entities involved in creating GAAP in the United States, it is a private, non-governmental organization.

   The _____ is subject to oversight by the Financial Accounting Foundation (FAF), which selects the members of the _____ and the Financial Accounting Standards Board, and funds both organizations.

   a. General partnership
   b. Depository Trust Company
   c. Wells Fargo ' Co.
   d. Governmental Accounting Standards Board

Chapter 11. Unique Aspects of Accounting for State and Local Governments

5. Two primary accounting methods, _____ and accrual basis, are used to calculate taxable income for U.S. federal income taxes. According to the Internal Revenue Code, a taxpayer may compute taxable income by:

   1. the Cash receipts and disbursements method;
   2. an accrual method;
   3. any other method permitted by the chapter; or
   4. any combination of the foregoing methods permitted under regulations prescribed by the Secretary.

As a general rule, a taxpayer must compute taxable income using the same accounting method he uses to compute income in keeping his books. Also, the taxpayer must maintain a consistent method of accounting from year to year. Should he change from the _____ to the accrual basis (or vice versa), he must notify and secure the consent of the Secretary.

   a. Cash basis
   b. 7-Eleven
   c. 529 plan
   d. 4-4-5 Calendar

6. A _____ (more commonly, _____) is a government financial statement, which goes beyond the minimums established for public sector companies by NCGA statement 1. Public sector companies will not have a statistical section in their Annual Financial Report (AFR) A _____ has three major sections : Introductory, financial, and statistical. The _____ is created with a showing offund accounting and Enterprise Authority accounting.
   a. 529 plan
   b. 4-4-5 Calendar
   c. Comprehensive Performance Assessment
   d. Comprehensive Annual Financial Report

7. _____ are formal records of a business' financial activities.

   _____ provide an overview of a business' financial condition in both short and long term. There are four basic _____:

   1. **Balance sheet**: also referred to as statement of financial position or condition, reports on a company's assets, liabilities, and net equity as of a given point in time.
   2. **Income statement**: also referred to as Profit and Loss statement (or a 'P'L'), reports on a company's income, expenses, and profits over a period of time.
   3. **Statement of retained earnings**: explains the changes in a company's retained earnings over the reporting period.
   4. **Statement of cash flows**: reports on a company's cash flow activities, particularly its operating, investing and financing activities.

Chapter 11. Unique Aspects of Accounting for State and Local Governments

a. Statement on Auditing Standards No. 70: Service Organizations
b. Statement of retained earnings
c. Notes to the Financial Statements
d. Financial statements

8. Accrual, in accounting, describes the accounting method known as _____, whereby revenues and expenses are recognized when they are accrued, i.e. accumulated (earned or incurred), regardless when the actual cash is received or paid out.

E.g. a company delivers a product to a customer who will pay for it 30 days later in the next fiscal year starting a week after the delivery. The company recognizes the proceeds as a revenue in its current income statement still for the fiscal year of the delivery, even though it will get paid in cash during the following accounting period.

a. ABN Amro
b. Accrual basis
c. A Random Walk Down Wall Street
d. AAB

9. Two primary _____, cash and accrual basis, and their combination, called modified cash basis, are used in recognizing income (revenues) and expenses in bookkeeping in order to measure net income for a specified time interval (accounting period.) Both methods differ on such recognition leading to varying income recordings, which may be subject to error or - manipulation. Many financial scandals involved accounting manipulations.

a. Accounting equation
b. Outstanding balance
c. Asset
d. Accounting methods

10. In business, _____ is income that a company receives from its normal business activities, usually from the sale of goods and services to customers. Some companies also receive _____ from interest, dividends or royalties paid to them by other companies. _____ may refer to business income in general, or it may refer to the amount, in a monetary unit, received during a period of time, as in 'Last year, Company X had _____ of $32 million.'

In many countries, including the UK, _____ is referred to as turnover.

a. Bottom line
b. Matching principle
c. Furniture, Fixtures and Equipment
d. Revenue

11. _____ is a legal term of art for anything that affects or limits the title of a property, such as mortgages, leases, easements, liens, or restrictions. Also, those considered as potentially making the title defeasible are also _____s. For example, charging orders, building orders and structure alteration.

a. A Random Walk Down Wall Street
b. Encumbrance
c. ABN Amro
d. AAB

12. _____ is the planning process used to determine whether a firm's long term investments such as new machinery, replacement machinery, new plants, new products, and research development projects are worth pursuing. It is budget for major capital, or investment, expenditures.

Many formal methods are used in _____, including the techniques such as

- Net present value
- Profitability index
- Internal rate of return
- Modified Internal Rate of Return
- Equivalent annuity

These methods use the incremental cash flows from each potential investment, or project. Techniques based on accounting earnings and accounting rules are sometimes used - though economists consider this to be improper - such as the accounting rate of return, and 'return on investment.' Simplified and hybrid methods are used as well, such as payback period and discounted payback period.

a. Shareholder value
b. Financial distress
c. Preferred stock
d. Capital budgeting

13. In the most general sense, a _____ is anything that is a hindrance, or puts individuals at a disadvantage.

Before we discuss the financial terms, we should note that a _____ can also have a much more important slang meaning.

This is best described in an example.

Chapter 11. Unique Aspects of Accounting for State and Local Governments 93

   a. Liability
   b. Covenant
   c. Limited liability
   d. McFadden Act

14. In economic models, the _____ time frame assumes no fixed factors of production. Firms can enter or leave the marketplace, and the cost (and availability) of land, labor, raw materials, and capital goods can be assumed to vary. In contrast, in the short-run time frame, certain factors are assumed to be fixed, because there is not sufficient time for them to change.
   a. 529 plan
   b. 4-4-5 Calendar
   c. Short-run
   d. Long-run

15. _____ are liabilities with a future benefit over one year, such as notes payable that mature greater than one year.

In accounting, the _____ are shown on the right wing of the balance-sheet representing the sources of funds, which are generally bounded in form of capital assets.

Examples of _____ are debentures, mortgage loans and other bank loans (note: not all bank loans are long term as not all are paid over a period greater than a year, the example is bridging loan.)

   a. Matching principle
   b. Deferred income
   c. Bottom line
   d. Long-term liabilities

16. _____ or financing is to provide capital (funds), which means money for a project, a person, a business or any other private or public institutions.

Those funds can be allocated for either short term or long term purposes. The health fund is a new way of _____ private healthcare centers.

   a. Product life cycle
   b. Synthetic CDO
   c. Proxy fight
   d. Funding

Chapter 11. Unique Aspects of Accounting for State and Local Governments

17. _____ plant, and equipment, is a term used in accountancy for assets and property which cannot easily be converted into cash. This can be compared with current assets such as cash or bank accounts, which are described as liquid assets. In most cases, only tangible assets are referred to as fixed.
    a. Fixed asset
    b. Percentage of Completion
    c. Remittance advice
    d. Petty cash

18. In business and accounting, _____s are everything of value that is owned by a person or company. The balance sheet of a firm records the monetary value of the _____s owned by the firm. The two major _____ classes are tangible _____s and intangible _____s.
    a. EBITDA
    b. Income
    c. Accounts payable
    d. Asset

19. _____ is that which is owed; usually referencing assets owed, but the term can cover other obligations. In the case of assets, _____ is a means of using future purchasing power in the present before a summation has been earned. Some companies and corporations use _____ as a part of their overall corporate finance strategy.
    a. Credit cycle
    b. Partial Payment
    c. Debt
    d. Cross-collateralization

20. The _____ duty is a legal relationship of confidence or trust between two or more parties, most commonly a _____ or trustee and a principal or beneficiary. One party, for example a corporate trust company or the trust department of a bank, holds a _____ relation or acts in a _____ capacity to another, such as one whose funds are entrusted to it for investment. In a _____ relation one person justifiably reposes confidence, good faith, reliance and trust in another whose aid, advice or protection is sought in some matter.
    a. Legal tender
    b. Fiduciary
    c. General obligation
    d. Financial Institutions Reform Recovery and Enforcement Act

Chapter 11. Unique Aspects of Accounting for State and Local Governments

21. In the United States, a _____ is one of the five fund types established by GAAP classified as a government fund, put simply a _____ may be used to generate and disperse money to those entitled to receive payments by qualification or agreement, as in the case of Alaska citizens or residents that satisfy the rules for payment from their permanet fund from State oil revenues. It was first introduced through GASB Statement 34. The name of the fund comes from the purpose of the fund: a sum of equity used to permanently generate payments to maintain some financial obligation.

   a. 529 plan
   b. 7-Eleven
   c. Permanent fund
   d. 4-4-5 Calendar

22. The phrase _____ refers to the aspect of corporate strategy, corporate finance and management dealing with the buying, selling and combining of different companies that can aid, finance, or help a growing company in a given industry grow rapidly without having to create another business entity.

An acquisition, also known as a takeover, is the buying of one company (the 'target') by another. An acquisition may be friendly or hostile.

   a. Mergers and acquisitions
   b. 529 plan
   c. 7-Eleven
   d. 4-4-5 Calendar

23. _____ is an accounting system often used by nonprofit organizations and by the public sector.

_____ serves any nonprofit organization or the public sector. These organizations have a need for special reporting to financial statements users that show how money is spent, rather than how much profit was earned.

   a. Bonus share
   b. Fund Accounting
   c. False billing
   d. Death spiral financing

24. _____ is the level of inventory that minimizes the total inventory holding costs and ordering costs. The framework used to determine this order quantity is also known as Wilson _____ Model. The model was developed by F. W. Harris in 1913.

Chapter 11. Unique Aspects of Accounting for State and Local Governments

a. AAB
b. A Random Walk Down Wall Street
c. ABN Amro
d. Economic order quantity

25. A _____ is a pool of assets forming an independent legal entity that are bought with the contributions to a pension plan for the exclusive purpose of financing pension plan benefits.

_____s are important shareholders of listed and private companies. They are especially important to the stock market where large institutional investors like the Ontario Teachers' Pension Plan dominate.

a. Leveraged buyout
b. Limited liability company
c. Pension fund
d. Leverage

26. _____ is a life of security. It may also refer to the final payment date of a loan or other financial instrument, at which point all remaining interest and principal is due to be paid.

1, 3, 6 months _____ band can be calculated by using 30-day per month periods.

a. False billing
b. Replacement cost
c. Primary market
d. Maturity

27. _____ are sometimes the same as net worth, or shareholders' equity - assets minus liabilities. The term _____ is commonly used with charities or not for profit entities. Although these entities don't make money, it is important to maintain reasonable reserves to help future growth.
a. Sharpe ratio
b. Sustainable growth rate
c. Cash conversion cycle
d. Net assets

Chapter 11. Unique Aspects of Accounting for State and Local Governments

28. The _____ is one of the basic financial statements as per Generally Accepted Accounting Principles, and it explains the changes in a company's retained earnings over the reporting period. It breaks down changes affecting the account, such as profits or losses from operations, dividends paid, and any other items charged or credited to retained earnings. A retained earnings statement is required by Generally Accepted Accounting Principles (GAAP) whenever comparative balance sheets and income statements are presented.

   a. Statement on Auditing Standards No. 70: Service Organizations
   b. Notes to the Financial Statements
   c. Financial statements
   d. Statement of retained earnings

29. _____ is a term used in accounting, economics and finance to spread the cost of an asset over the span of several years.

In simple words we can say that _____ is the reduction in the value of an asset due to usage, passage of time, wear and tear, technological outdating or obsolescence, depletion or other such factors.

In accounting, _____ is a term used to describe any method of attributing the historical or purchase cost of an asset across its useful life, roughly corresponding to normal wear and tear.

   a. Depreciation
   b. Deferred financing costs
   c. Bottom line
   d. Matching principle

Chapter 12. Financial Statement Analysis

1. _____ is the standard framework of guidelines for financial accounting used in the United States of America. It includes the standards, conventions, and rules accountants follow in recording and summarizing transactions, and in the preparation of financial statements. _____ are now issued by the Financial Accounting Standards Board (FASB).
    a. Depreciation
    b. Net income
    c. Revenue
    d. Generally Accepted Accounting Principles

2. In finance, _____ is the ability of an entity to pay its debts with available cash. _____ can also be described as the ability of a corporation to meet its long-term fixed expenses and to accomplish long-term expansion and growth. The better a company's _____, the better it is financially.
    a. Capital asset
    b. Solvency
    c. Political risk
    d. Mid price

3. _____ are formal records of a business' financial activities.

    _____ provide an overview of a business' financial condition in both short and long term. There are four basic _____:

    1. **Balance sheet**: also referred to as statement of financial position or condition, reports on a company's assets, liabilities, and net equity as of a given point in time.
    2. **Income statement**: also referred to as Profit and Loss statement (or a 'P'L'), reports on a company's income, expenses, and profits over a period of time.
    3. **Statement of retained earnings**: explains the changes in a company's retained earnings over the reporting period.
    4. **Statement of cash flows**: reports on a company's cash flow activities, particularly its operating, investing and financing activities.

    a. Notes to the Financial Statements
    b. Financial statements
    c. Statement of retained earnings
    d. Statement on Auditing Standards No. 70: Service Organizations

4. In financial accounting, a _____ or statement of financial position is a summary of a person's or organization's balances. Assets, liabilities and ownership equity are listed as of a specific date, such as the end of its financial year. A _____ is often described as a snapshot of a company's financial condition.

Chapter 12. Financial Statement Analysis

a. Statement on Auditing Standards No. 70: Service Organizations
b. Financial statements
c. Statement of retained earnings
d. Balance sheet

5. _____ is the balance of the amounts of cash being received and paid by a business during a defined period of time, sometimes tied to a specific project. Measurement of _____ can be used

- to evaluate the state or performance of a business or project.
- to determine problems with liquidity. Being profitable does not necessarily mean being liquid. A company can fail because of a shortage of cash, even while profitable.
- to generate project rate of returns. The time of _____s into and out of projects are used as inputs to financial models such as internal rate of return, and net present value.
- to examine income or growth of a business when it is believed that accrual accounting concepts do not represent economic realities. Alternately, _____ can be used to 'validate' the net income generated by accrual accounting.

_____ as a generic term may be used differently depending on context, and certain _____ definitions may be adapted by analysts and users for their own uses. Common terms include operating _____ and free _____.

_____s can be classified into:

1. Operational _____s: Cash received or expended as a result of the company's core business activities.
2. Investment _____s: Cash received or expended through capital expenditure, investments or acquisitions.
3. Financing _____s: Cash received or expended as a result of financial activities, such as interests and dividends.

All three together - the net _____ - are necessary to reconcile the beginning cash balance to the ending cash balance. Loan draw downs or equity injections, that is just shifting of capital but no expenditure as such, are not considered in the net _____.

a. Shareholder value
b. Cash flow
c. Corporate finance
d. Real option

6. In financial accounting, a _____ or statement of cash flows is a financial statement that shows a company's flow of cash. The money coming into the business is called cash inflow, and money going out from the business is called cash outflow. The statement shows how changes in balance sheet and income accounts affect cash and cash equivalents, and breaks the analysis down to operating, investing, and financing activities.

a. 7-Eleven
b. 4-4-5 Calendar
c. Cash flow statement
d. 529 plan

7. _____ is a list for goods and materials held available in stock by a business. It is also used for a list of the contents of a household and for a list for testamentary purposes of the possessions of someone who has died. In accounting _____ is considered an asset.

a. A Random Walk Down Wall Street
b. ABN Amro
c. Inventory
d. AAB

8. _____ are securities that can be easily converted into cash. Such securities will generally have highly liquid markets allowing the security to be sold at a reasonable price very quickly. This is a usual feature in real estate .

a. Marketable
b. Securities lending
c. Book entry
d. Tracking stock

9. A _____ is a fungible, negotiable instrument representing financial value. They are broadly categorized into debt securities (such as banknotes, bonds and debentures), and equity securities; e.g., common stocks. The company or other entity issuing the _____ is called the issuer.

a. Book entry
b. Tracking stock
c. Securities lending
d. Security

10. _____ are liabilities that may or may not be incurred by an entity depending on the outcome of a future event such as a court case. These liabilities are recorded in a company's accounts and shown in the balance sheet when both probable and reasonably estimable. A footnote to the balance sheet describes the nature and extent of the _____.

a. Due-on-sale clause
b. 4-4-5 Calendar
c. 529 plan
d. Contingent liabilities

Chapter 12. Financial Statement Analysis

11. In economics, a _____ is a type of retirement plan in which the amount of the employer's annual contribution is specified. Individual accounts are set up for participants and benefits are based on the amounts credited to these accounts (through employer contributions and, if applicable, employee contributions) plus any investment earnings on the money in the account. Only employer contributions to the account are guaranteed, not the future benefits. In _____s, future benefits fluctuate on the basis of investment earnings.

   a. Defined contribution plan
   b. Fixed asset turnover
   c. Capital costs
   d. Total revenue

12. In the most general sense, a _____ is anything that is a hindrance, or puts individuals at a disadvantage.

Before we discuss the financial terms, we should note that a _____ can also have a much more important slang meaning.

This is best described in an example.

   a. Limited liability
   b. Liability
   c. Covenant
   d. McFadden Act

13. The _____ is a financial ratio that measures whether or not a firm has enough resources to pay its debts over the next 12 months. It compares a firm's current assets to its current liabilities. It is expressed as follows:

$$\text{Current ratio} = \frac{\text{Current Assets}}{\text{Current Liabilities}}$$

For example, if WXY Company's current assets are $50,000,000 and its current liabilities are $40,000,000, then its _____ would be $50,000,000 divided by $40,000,000, which equals 1.25.

   a. Sustainable growth rate
   b. PEG ratio
   c. Debt service coverage ratio
   d. Current ratio

14. _____ is a measure of the ability of a debtor to pay their debts as and when they fall due. It is usually expressed as a ratio or a percentage of current liabilities.

Chapter 12. Financial Statement Analysis

For a corporation with a published balance sheet there are various ratios used to calculate a measure of liquidity.

a. Operating leverage
b. Invested capital
c. Accounting liquidity
d. Operating profit margin

15. In finance, the Acid-test or _____ or liquid ratio measures the ability of a company to use its near cash or quick assets to immediately extinguish or retire its current liabilities. Quick assets include those current assets that presumably can be quickly converted to cash at close to their book values.

Generally, the acid test ratio should be 1:1 or better, however this varies widely by industry.

a. Financial ratio
b. P/E ratio
c. Quick ratio
d. Net assets

16. _____ plant, and equipment, is a term used in accountancy for assets and property which cannot easily be converted into cash. This can be compared with current assets such as cash or bank accounts, which are described as liquid assets. In most cases, only tangible assets are referred to as fixed.

a. Fixed asset
b. Percentage of Completion
c. Remittance advice
d. Petty cash

17. _____ is the ratio of sales (on the Profit and loss account) to the value of fixed assets (on the balance sheet.) It indicates how well the business is using its fixed assets to generate sales.

Generally speaking, the higher the ratio, the better, because a high ratio indicates the business has less money tied up in fixed assets for each dollar of sales revenue.

a. Total revenue
b. Market microstructure
c. Defined contribution plan
d. Fixed asset turnover

18. The _____ is an equation that equals the cost of goods sold divided by the average inventory. Average inventory equals beginning inventory plus ending inventory divided by 2.

The formula for _____:

$$\text{Inventory Turnover} = \frac{\text{Cost of Goods Sold}}{\text{Average Inventory}}$$

The formula for average inventory:

$$\text{Average Inventory} = \frac{\text{Beginning inventory} + \text{Ending inventory}}{2}$$

A low turnover rate may point to overstocking, obsolescence, or deficiencies in the product line or marketing effort.

a. Inventory turnover
b. Operating leverage
c. Earnings yield
d. Information ratio

19. In business and accounting, _____s are everything of value that is owned by a person or company. The balance sheet of a firm records the monetary value of the _____s owned by the firm. The two major _____ classes are tangible _____s and intangible _____s.
a. Asset
b. Accounts payable
c. Income
d. EBITDA

20. _____ is a financial ratio that measures the efficiency of a company's use of its assets in generating sales revenue or sales income to the company.

Chapter 12. Financial Statement Analysis

$$Asset\ Turnover = \frac{Sales}{Average\ Total\ Assets}$$

- 'Sales' is the value of 'Net Sales' or 'Sales' from the company's income statement
- 'Average Total Assets' is the value of 'Total assets' from the company's balance sheet in the beginning and the end of the fiscal period divided by 2.

- Assets turnover

a. Average accounting return
b. Inventory turnover
c. Earnings yield
d. Asset turnover

21. In finance, _____ (or gearing) is borrowing money to supplement existing funds for investment in such a way that the potential positive or negative outcome is magnified and/or enhanced. It generally refers to using borrowed funds, or debt, so as to attempt to increase the returns to equity. Deleveraging is the action of reducing borrowings.
    a. Financial endowment
    b. Limited partnership
    c. Pension fund
    d. Leverage

22. _____ is that which is owed; usually referencing assets owed, but the term can cover other obligations. In the case of assets, _____ is a means of using future purchasing power in the present before a summation has been earned. Some companies and corporations use _____ as a part of their overall corporate finance strategy.
    a. Partial Payment
    b. Debt
    c. Credit cycle
    d. Cross-collateralization

23. _____ is a financial ratio that indicates the percentage of a company's assets are provided via debt. It is the ratio of total debt (the sum of current liabilities and long-term liabilities) and total assets (the sum of current assets, fixed assets, and other assets such as 'goodwill'.)

or alternatively:

For example, a company with $2 million in total assets and $500,000 in total liabilities would have a _____ of 25%

Like all financial ratios, a company's _____ should be compared with their industry average or other competing firms.

a. Capitalization rate
b. Cash management
c. Debt ratio
d. Cash concentration

24. In business, operating margin, operating income margin, _____ or return on sales (ROS) is the ratio of operating income (operating profit in the UK) divided by net sales, usually presented in percent.

(Relevant figures in italics)

It is a measurement of what proportion of a company's revenue is left over, before taxes and other indirect costs (such as rent, bonus, interest, etc.), after paying for variable costs of production as wages, raw materials, etc. A good operating margin is needed for a company to be able to pay for its fixed costs, such as interest on debt.

a. Interest coverage ratio
b. Average rate of return
c. Operating leverage
d. Operating profit margin

25. The _____ percentage shows how profitable a company's assets are in generating revenue.

_____ can be computed as:

Chapter 12. Financial Statement Analysis

$$ROA = \frac{\text{Net Income}}{\text{Total Assets}}$$

This number tells you 'what the company can do with what it's got', i.e. how many dollars of earnings they derive from each dollar of assets they control. It's a useful number for comparing competing companies in the same industry.

a. Return on sales
b. Receivables turnover ratio
c. Return on assets
d. P/E ratio

26. _____ measures the rate of return on the ownership interest (shareholders' equity) of the common stock owners. _____ is viewed as one of the most important financial ratios. It measures a firm's efficiency at generating profits from every dollar of shareholders' equity (also known as net assets or assets minus liabilities.)

a. Return on equity
b. Diluted Earnings Per Share
c. Return on sales
d. Return of capital

27. In finance, a _____ is collateral that the holder of a position in securities, options, or futures contracts has to deposit to cover the credit risk of his counterparty (most often his broker.) This risk can arise if the holder has done any of the following:

- borrowed cash from the counterparty to buy securities or options,
- sold securities or options short, or
- entered into a futures contract.

The collateral can be in the form of cash or securities, and it is deposited in a _____ account. On U.S. futures exchanges, '_____' was formally called performance bond.

_____ buying is buying securities with cash borrowed from a broker, using other securities as collateral.

a. Share
b. Procter ' Gamble
c. Margin
d. Credit

28. _____ are sometimes the same as net worth, or shareholders' equity - assets minus liabilities. The term _____ is commonly used with charities or not for profit entities. Although these entities don't make money, it is important to maintain reasonable reserves to help future growth.
   a. Cash conversion cycle
   b. Sustainable growth rate
   c. Sharpe ratio
   d. Net assets

Chapter 13. Financial Condition Analysis

1. _____ are formal records of a business' financial activities.

_____ provide an overview of a business' financial condition in both short and long term. There are four basic _____:

   1. **Balance sheet**: also referred to as statement of financial position or condition, reports on a company's assets, liabilities, and net equity as of a given point in time.
   2. **Income statement**: also referred to as Profit and Loss statement (or a 'P'L'), reports on a company's income, expenses, and profits over a period of time.
   3. **Statement of retained earnings**: explains the changes in a company's retained earnings over the reporting period.
   4. **Statement of cash flows**: reports on a company's cash flow activities, particularly its operating, investing and financing activities.

   a. Statement of retained earnings
   b. Notes to the Financial Statements
   c. Financial statements
   d. Statement on Auditing Standards No. 70: Service Organizations

2. _____ is a legally declared inability or impairment of ability of an individual or organization to pay their creditors. Creditors may file a _____ petition against a debtor ('involuntary _____') in an effort to recoup a portion of what they are owed or initiate a restructuring. In the majority of cases, however, _____ is initiated by the debtor (a 'voluntary _____' that is filed by the bankrupt individual or organization.)
   a. Debt settlement
   b. Bankruptcy
   c. 529 plan
   d. 4-4-5 Calendar

3. A _____ (more commonly, _____) is a government financial statement, which goes beyond the minimums established for public sector companies by NCGA statement 1. Public sector companies will not have a statistical section in their Annual Financial Report (AFR) A _____ has three major sections : Introductory, financial, and statistical. The _____ is created with a showing offund accounting and Enterprise Authority accounting.
   a. Comprehensive Performance Assessment
   b. Comprehensive Annual Financial Report
   c. 529 plan
   d. 4-4-5 Calendar

4. _____ is the standard framework of guidelines for financial accounting used in the United States of America. It includes the standards, conventions, and rules accountants follow in recording and summarizing transactions, and in the preparation of financial statements. _____ are now issued by the Financial Accounting Standards Board (FASB).

a. Generally Accepted Accounting Principles
b. Net income
c. Revenue
d. Depreciation

5. The role of the _____ is to issue accounting standards in the United Kingdom. It is recognised for that purpose under the Companies Act 1985. It took over the task of setting accounting standards from the Accounting Standards Committee (ASC) in 1990.
   a. Accounting Standards Board
   b. ABN Amro
   c. A Random Walk Down Wall Street
   d. AAB

6. Accrual, in accounting, describes the accounting method known as _____, whereby revenues and expenses are recognized when they are accrued, i.e. accumulated (earned or incurred), regardless when the actual cash is received or paid out.

E.g. a company delivers a product to a customer who will pay for it 30 days later in the next fiscal year starting a week after the delivery. The company recognizes the proceeds as a revenue in its current income statement still for the fiscal year of the delivery, even though it will get paid in cash during the following accounting period.

   a. AAB
   b. A Random Walk Down Wall Street
   c. Accrual basis
   d. ABN Amro

7. _____ is an umbrella term which refers to the various accounting systems used by various public sector entities. In the United States, for instance, there are three levels of government which follow different accounting standards set forth by independent, private sector boards. At the federal level, the Federal Accounting Standards Advisory Board (FASAB) sets forth the accounting standards to follow.
   a. Governmental Accounting
   b. Management accounting
   c. Grenzplankostenrechnung
   d. Nonassurance services

8. The _____ is currently the source of generally accepted accounting principles (GAAP) used by State and Local governments in the United States of America. As with most of the entities involved in creating GAAP in the United States, it is a private, non-governmental organization.

Chapter 13. Financial Condition Analysis

The _____ is subject to oversight by the Financial Accounting Foundation (FAF), which selects the members of the _____ and the Financial Accounting Standards Board, and funds both organizations.

a. Wells Fargo ' Co.
b. General partnership
c. Depository Trust Company
d. Governmental Accounting Standards Board

9. Two primary _____, cash and accrual basis, and their combination, called modified cash basis, are used in recognizing income (revenues) and expenses in bookkeeping in order to measure net income for a specified time interval (accounting period.) Both methods differ on such recognition leading to varying income recordings, which may be subject to error or - manipulation. Many financial scandals involved accounting manipulations.

a. Accounting equation
b. Outstanding balance
c. Asset
d. Accounting methods

10. _____ is a measure of the ability of a debtor to pay their debts as and when they fall due. It is usually expressed as a ratio or a percentage of current liabilities.

For a corporation with a published balance sheet there are various ratios used to calculate a measure of liquidity.

a. Operating profit margin
b. Operating leverage
c. Invested capital
d. Accounting liquidity

11. In finance, _____ is the ability of an entity to pay its debts with available cash. _____ can also be described as the ability of a corporation to meet its long-term fixed expenses and to accomplish long-term expansion and growth. The better a company's _____, the better it is financially.

a. Mid price
b. Political risk
c. Solvency
d. Capital asset

Chapter 13. Financial Condition Analysis

12. _____ is that which is owed; usually referencing assets owed, but the term can cover other obligations. In the case of assets, _____ is a means of using future purchasing power in the present before a summation has been earned. Some companies and corporations use _____ as a part of their overall corporate finance strategy.
    a. Partial Payment
    b. Credit cycle
    c. Cross-collateralization
    d. Debt

13. _____ is the level of inventory that minimizes the total inventory holding costs and ordering costs. The framework used to determine this order quantity is also known as Wilson _____ Model. The model was developed by F. W. Harris in 1913.
    a. ABN Amro
    b. AAB
    c. A Random Walk Down Wall Street
    d. Economic order quantity

14. In finance, _____ (or gearing) is borrowing money to supplement existing funds for investment in such a way that the potential positive or negative outcome is magnified and/or enhanced. It generally refers to using borrowed funds, or debt, so as to attempt to increase the returns to equity. Deleveraging is the action of reducing borrowings.
    a. Financial endowment
    b. Pension fund
    c. Limited partnership
    d. Leverage

15. _____ is the amount by which a reference rate is multiplied to determine the floating interest rate payable by an inverse floater. Some debt instruments leverage the particular effects of interest rate changes, most commonly in inverse floaters.

As an example, an inverse floater with a multiple may pay interest at the rate of 22 percent minus the product of 2 times the 1-month London Interbank Offered Rate (LIBOR.)

    a. Coupon leverage
    b. Trade date
    c. Gross spread
    d. Systematic risk

16. _____ is an accounting system often used by nonprofit organizations and by the public sector.

Chapter 13. Financial Condition Analysis

_____ serves any nonprofit organization or the public sector. These organizations have a need for special reporting to financial statements users that show how money is spent, rather than how much profit was earned.

a. Bonus share
b. Death spiral financing
c. Fund Accounting
d. False billing

17. In economic models, the _____ time frame assumes no fixed factors of production. Firms can enter or leave the marketplace, and the cost (and availability) of land, labor, raw materials, and capital goods can be assumed to vary. In contrast, in the short-run time frame, certain factors are assumed to be fixed, because there is not sufficient time for them to change.

a. 529 plan
b. 4-4-5 Calendar
c. Short-run
d. Long-run

18. A _____ or equity fund is a fund that invests in Equities more commonly known as stocks. Such funds are typically held either in stock or cash, as opposed to Bonds, notes, or other securities. This may be a mutual fund or exchange-traded fund.

a. Mutual fund fees and expenses
b. Stock fund
c. Money market funds
d. Closed-end fund

19. The phrase _____ refers to the aspect of corporate strategy, corporate finance and management dealing with the buying, selling and combining of different companies that can aid, finance, or help a growing company in a given industry grow rapidly without having to create another business entity.

An acquisition, also known as a takeover, is the buying of one company (the 'target') by another. An acquisition may be friendly or hostile.

a. 4-4-5 Calendar
b. 529 plan
c. Mergers and acquisitions
d. 7-Eleven

Chapter 13. Financial Condition Analysis

20. In finance, a _____ is a debt security, in which the authorized issuer owes the holders a debt and, depending on the terms of the _____, is obliged to pay interest (the coupon) and/or to repay the principal at a later date, termed maturity.

Thus a _____ is a loan: the issuer is the borrower, the _____ holder is the lender, and the coupon is the interest. _____s provide the borrower with external funds to finance long-term investments, or, in the case of government _____s, to finance current expenditure.

a. Convertible bond
b. Puttable bond
c. Catastrophe bonds
d. Bond

21. _____ is a fee paid on borrowed assets. It is the price paid for the use of borrowed money , or, money earned by deposited funds . Assets that are sometimes lent with _____ include money, shares, consumer goods through hire purchase, major assets such as aircraft, and even entire factories in finance lease arrangements.

a. AAB
b. Insolvency
c. A Random Walk Down Wall Street
d. Interest

22. In economics, business, and accounting, a _____ is the value of money that has been used up to produce something, and hence is not available for use anymore. In business, the _____ may be one of acquisition, in which case the amount of money expended to acquire it is counted as _____. In this case, money is the input that is gone in order to acquire the thing.

a. Fixed costs
b. Sliding scale fees
c. Marginal cost
d. Cost

23. In finance, a _____ (non-investment grade bond, speculative grade bond or junk bond) is a bond that is rated below investment grade at the time of purchase. These bonds have a higher risk of default or other adverse credit events, but typically pay higher yields than better quality bonds in order to make them attractive to investors.

a. Sharpe ratio
b. Volatility
c. Private equity
d. High yield bond

Chapter 1
1. d 2. d 3. d 4. d 5. c 6. d 7. c 8. d 9. a 10. d
11. d 12. b 13. d 14. a 15. d 16. d 17. b

Chapter 2
1. d 2. b 3. d 4. d 5. d 6. d 7. d 8. b 9. d 10. a
11. a 12. c 13. b 14. d 15. a 16. d 17. c 18. c

Chapter 3
1. a 2. b 3. d 4. d 5. b 6. a 7. d 8. d 9. a 10. b
11. d 12. d 13. b 14. a 15. c 16. d 17. b 18. c 19. d 20. d
21. d 22. d 23. b 24. d 25. c 26. b 27. d 28. d 29. d

Chapter 4
1. a 2. d 3. c 4. a 5. a 6. a 7. a 8. d 9. b 10. d
11. d 12. c 13. d 14. b

Chapter 5
1. a 2. c 3. d 4. b 5. c 6. a 7. d 8. d 9. b 10. d
11. d 12. d 13. a 14. b 15. a 16. d 17. b 18. d 19. b 20. d
21. d 22. a 23. d 24. d 25. a 26. d 27. d 28. d 29. d 30. b
31. d 32. a 33. b 34. d 35. a 36. b 37. d 38. d 39. c 40. d
41. a 42. c 43. b 44. d 45. b 46. a

Chapter 6
1. b 2. d 3. c 4. c 5. a 6. d 7. d 8. b 9. c 10. d
11. d 12. c 13. d 14. d 15. d 16. d 17. d 18. d 19. d 20. a
21. a 22. b 23. d 24. d 25. a 26. a 27. d 28. d 29. a 30. d
31. d 32. a 33. d 34. d

Chapter 7
1. b 2. a 3. d 4. d 5. d 6. c 7. d 8. d 9. d 10. d
11. d 12. d 13. a 14. c

Chapter 8
1. a 2. b 3. d 4. c 5. d 6. d 7. d 8. d 9. d 10. b
11. d 12. d 13. c 14. d 15. d 16. d 17. d 18. d 19. c 20. b
21. d 22. d 23. a 24. a 25. a 26. b 27. d 28. d 29. d 30. a
31. d 32. d 33. a 34. d 35. b 36. c 37. d 38. b 39. a 40. c
41. d 42. d 43. c 44. c 45. a 46. d 47. b 48. d 49. d 50. d
51. d 52. d 53. b 54. a 55. d

Chapter 9
1. a 2. d 3. b 4. d 5. a 6. c 7. d 8. c 9. c 10. d
11. d 12. a 13. d 14. b 15. d 16. d 17. d 18. d 19. c 20. d
21. d 22. d 23. d 24. a 25. b 26. d 27. c 28. a

ANSWER KEY

Chapter 10
1. d   2. a   3. d   4. d   5. c   6. d   7. d   8. c   9. c   10. d
11. d   12. d   13. b   14. d

Chapter 11
1. d   2. d   3. b   4. d   5. a   6. d   7. d   8. b   9. d   10. d
11. b   12. d   13. a   14. d   15. d   16. d   17. a   18. d   19. c   20. b
21. c   22. a   23. b   24. d   25. c   26. d   27. d   28. d   29. a

Chapter 12
1. d   2. b   3. b   4. d   5. b   6. c   7. c   8. a   9. d   10. d
11. a   12. b   13. d   14. c   15. c   16. a   17. d   18. a   19. a   20. d
21. d   22. b   23. c   24. d   25. c   26. a   27. c   28. d

Chapter 13
1. c   2. b   3. b   4. a   5. a   6. c   7. a   8. d   9. d   10. d
11. c   12. d   13. d   14. d   15. a   16. c   17. d   18. b   19. c   20. d
21. d   22. d   23. d